Sleep
& Grow
Rich

TITLES BY GARY S. GOODMAN

Sleep & Grow Rich

―∞―

DR. GARY S. GOODMAN

MEDIA

Published 2020 by Gildan Media LLC
aka G&D Media
www.GandDmedia.com

First Edition: 2020

Front cover design by David Rheinhardt of Pyrographx

Interior design by Meghan Day Healey of Story Horse, LLC.

Library of Congress Cataloging-in-Publication Data is available upon request

ISBN: 978-1-7225-0325-3

10   9   8   7   6   5   4   3   2   1

Contents

Introduction

How to Become the Richest Person in the World

What does it take to become the richest person in the world? What would you say? Most people would say hard work, cleverness, persistence, a dose of good luck, and possibly choosing the right parents.

If we ask the actual person occupying that top spot, the one who currently is capitalism's biggest winner, the richest man in the world today, what does he say? Jeff Bezos, founder and guiding light behind the trillion-dollar Amazon, says one of his key practices is *sleeping*.

Here's how he explained it recently, to the *Wall Street Journal*:

> "I go to bed early, I get up early, I like to putter in the morning" reading the newspaper, drink-

ing a cup of coffee and eating breakfast with his children, he said. Mr. Bezos schedules "high IQ" meetings before lunch, and tries to finish making his tough decisions by 5 PM.

Mr. Bezos said his primary job each day as a senior executive is to make a small number of high-quality decisions. That means getting eight hours of sleep, too. "I think better, I have more energy, my mood's better," he said.

If he slept less, he could make more decisions. "But it wouldn't be worth it."

Sleeping Habits of Geniuses

As she does every morning, my wife asks, "How did you sleep?" Her next question is, "Did you have dreams?" I dreamed she was driving a vintage Bentley convertible, top down, and I was reaching from the passenger seat to help her to steer into a left turn in an upscale residential neighborhood. A beautiful day in a dreamy ride with top down and happy riders: What could be better?

Later, after dropping one of my ballerinas off to her class, I was reading at the library and it hit me. The true way to wealth and a signature of having arrived at real luxury is the ability to *sleep through the night,* and to *nap-at-will.* If Norman Rockwell could re-title his suite of iconic paintings, he'd call them the Five Freedoms. In addition to freedom of speech, freedom of worship, freedom from want and freedom from fear, there would be the freedom to sleep.

But wait a second. As I researched these paintings, I noticed something tremendously important. The third, freedom from fear, depicts parents tucking their children into bed, memorializing the centrality of sleep in our pantheon of freedoms.

In America, we celebrate those that have the backbone to toil long hours and to limit their shut-eye. Indeed, this all-work-no-sleep ethic permeates our self-help literature. Stories are told about Thomas Edison, who purportedly never slept at length. It was his ongoing, relentless focus that led to an extraordinary number of patents. To this day I pay a company called Southern California Edison for my electric bill.

You might gather from how the sleepless-Edison tale is told that his lack of sleep caused or at least facilitated his inventiveness. I am here to say this folklore is wrong. Edison was a magnificent sleeper! He slept many times a day, in what we call naps. He was able to refresh himself this way because, according to some scientists, it isn't how long we sleep that matters, but how deeply we sleep when we shove off into that nether world. If Edison was able to reach the deepest level of sleep consciousness multiple times a day, he was a far more accomplished sleeper than those sleeping longer but more superficially.

The idea that "Edison never slept!" is an utter fiction. I'm very fond of Edison-prevarications. In one of my most-viewed online articles, *Exactly, How*

Many Times Did Edison Fail? I share my research into the inventor and especially this myth about his failures.

Estimates vary wildly, yet unlike numerous inventors, Edison died rich, leaving an estate of $12 million in 1931. This is worth more than $187 million today.

Literally, Edison slept and grew rich.

You could say he slept his way to a great fortune. I realize this is punctuating his work style in an unusual manner, but it is more plausible an explanation than asserting he never slept. Sleeping, or napping if you like, was central to his capacity to invent numerous devices that changed the world. Yet we imagine him and other moguls as insomniacs.

My argument is that the poorest people on the planet are the most sleep deprived. They are also among the nuttiest, the least stable, and the least healthy.

If you want to be happy, productive and rich, or at least feel like it most of the time, get a good night's sleep. And if that doesn't do it, sleep some more! If someone brings you a wonderful sounding business proposition, or a magnificent offer of any kind, what is the best advice you can hear? Sleep on it. We are told this is sage advice because letting a sizzling offer cool off for 24 hours is a good way of not getting hustled. We show down the transaction, and if we're being conned, the miscreant might slip into the night. And we might realize things that sound too good to be true are often just that. People have saved, which is to say they have made, billions of dollars, by following this advice.

Sleeping on something engages our unconscious, and this is why it is so valuable to permit a cooling off period. If we have nightmares or just a fitful reaction to the offer that prevents us from sleeping, this could be an authentic "danger" message from our inner self. We could be tapping a source inside ourselves that is alert to tiny nuances that our conscious being wasn't aware of when we were awake.

I took my happy-go-lucky Doberman pinscher to a real estate transaction I was doing. Meeting me at the property was my buyer and his building contractor. The buyer made a verbal offer that was less than half what I was asking. Blue, my dog, growled when he heard it.

"Is he growling at me?" the suddenly flustered buyer asked.

Blue never growled. He didn't bite, either. He was a wonderful dog bereft of gifts other than affection. But on that occasion he picked up on something I had missed entirely. The buyer was a sleaze, someone to avoid doing business with. We have our own inner Blues. These are the signals sent from our sleeping state to our conscious beings. They warn us, and they can also make us rich.

Einstein had a dream he was riding on a beam of light and this ignited his interest in relativity theory, which has certainly enriched humanity. His dream and subsequent mining of its meaning made him rich. He died with a fortune of $10 million in today's dollars, was the country's top paid professor at Princeton, and his heirs continue to earn a reported $12 million from his name, image, and publications.

Another inventive fellow who slept and grew rich!

These bright luminaries, Edison and Einstein, had to recharge their batteries to accomplish what they did when the sun came up. They're given credit for the results, but not for the precursory and necessary antecedent, sleeping.

The Sleep Deprived
Are Among the Poorest,
Unhealthiest & Most
Dangerous People on Earth

———∽∞∾———

What we know about *sleep-poverty is* simply astonishing.

Highway deaths are caused by drowsy drivers more often than by drunk and drugged drivers. This is especially a problem for long-distance truckers and professional roadsters of various types, like cabbies.

The sleep deprived live shorter, more diseased lives than folks that get the proper amount. Research done by the University of California at Berkeley shows there may be a causal link between getting less sleep and the onset of Alzheimer's disease.

We downplay the importance of the typical symptoms of sleepy heads. Irritability, slowness of thought and physical reflexes, are just a few.

Coffee is the second most widely traded commodity in the world. Its increasing usage is responsible for impaired and reduced sleep, ironically, as it is used to compensate for these problems.

Sleep deprivation also makes us fatter. We eat more when we sleep less.

When you add up all of the physical and social costs of sleeplessness, it is astonishing that we haven't declared an epidemic and sought to remedy the situation.

ELON MUSK: THE MARLBORO MAN OF SLEEPLESSNESS

Do you remember The Marlboro Man? This was a cowboy figure used to sell Marlboro cigarettes in advertising campaigns from 1954–1999. That icon of virility was a likely factor in millions of lives being lost to lung cancer. When the Marlboro Man campaign was started, sales were at $5 billion. Two years later, sales were at $20 billion, representing a 300% increase. Four of the male models used in Marlboro ads died prematurely, of lung related diseases.

We lionize people that seem to tough things out. Despite behaviors that are self-defeating, we still give them a heroic aura. This especially applies to those boasting they can get along on less sleep.

Elon Musk is a generally well-respected innovator in business, the force behind several companies including Tesla and Space X. He boasted about his purposeful lack of sleep. According to one psychologist, Musk has not benefited from his deprivation.

In an article titled, *Here's Why Your's & Elon Musk's Lack of Sleep is Bad,* John M. Grohol, Psy.D comments:

> "If you wonder what lack of sleep looks like, look no further than business magnate Elon Musk and his erratic behavior over the past few months. From believing that he alone had the time and unique resources to save the Thai boys trapped in a cave to prematurely tweeting that he had 'funding secured' (when he didn't) for a private buyout of Tesla, his embattled electric car company, Musk has shown a troubling pattern of ignoring his own self-care."

Musk is the Marlboro Man of sleeplessness. He makes it sound good and look heroic, but a serious lack of shut-eye isn't working for him, or really, for anyone else. Yet the idea is charismatic, the lone cowboy innovator sacrificing his body for commercial advancement and technological immortality.

WHAT DO MILLIONAIRES GAIN IF THEY LOSE THEIR SLEEP?

For argument sake, let's say sacrificing two hours of sleep each day liberates 60 hours of working time per month and 720 hours annually that you can apply to making money. However, it shortens your life in actual number of years lived and it diminishes your health, while making you grumpy. Sleeplessness makes you poor now, emotionally and physically, and dead sooner. How can this be a good deal?

Before a convention assembly, when my dad asked to share the secret of his success in selling, he declared:

"The early bird gets the worm; it's true. But that all he gets—worms!"

He went on to say he sleeps in until 9 or 9:30 every morning. Eats a full, leisurely breakfast, and then he decides if he wants to sell that day. If he's not in the mood, he simply doesn't bother. His road weary fellow salespeople broke out in applause. They loved dad's candor. But management hated it because it violated the work ethic we are pushed to uphold in business.

Working yourself to death is a prized form of suicide in America. As Dr. Grohol puts it:

"Lack of sleep can literally kill you sooner."

Much is made today about achieving a work-life balance. Aristotle called it the golden mean, a moderate position between two extremes, between too much and not enough. A good and necessary first step to achieving this is to strive for sleep-and-awake balance. Let me be perfectly clear. I am saying that by sleeping less, we diminish our chances of developing objectively measured wealth, what we think of as money-wealth. Additionally, we are becoming poorer by making ourselves miserable in the meantime.

Sleep Better & Be Better Now!

When you are well rested, you're more likely to have this epiphany—*you are actually rich right now*. Nothing is lacking. You are energetic, rejuvenated, restored, and reset. It's like being on vacation without having to catch tour buses or hear island music. When you embrace this idea that you are rich right now, you're far more likely to develop objective wealth than by feeling needy or having a sense of lacking.

Recently, I was riding along with some slumping salespeople. One of them was a new dad of an 11-month old. Having been there not long ago with two infants of my own, I was definitely sleep deprived at the time.

Saying a salesperson is in a slump is usually a metaphorical reference that means their sales are down. But when we're sleep deprived, we *physically* slump. Our shoulders droop along with our eyelids

and our paychecks. This suggests to would-be buyers that we're less than enthusiastic about how our
products will perform. Fearing they'll be slumping
too, prospects are wary of buying. Thus a cycle of
non-selling is started and perpetuated.

Before entering a house in an affluent area, I
whispered to my trainee, the new papa:

"We're rich. We don't need this sale, though we'd
like to get it and we deserve to get it."

I said this as an antidote to pressing, to struggling, which is what slumping sellers typically do.
He relaxed, getting my meaning instantly. And he
earned the deal. I repeated this mantra with other
slumpers under my wing. Their sales soared, too.

THE LIE WE BUY IS THAT WE CAN DEPRIVE OURSELVES TO A GREAT FORTUNE

Work backbreaking hours, toiling at something you
hate, and after a decade or two or three, you'll be on
easy street, right?

Wrong! Recently, I found a great discussion
among some of the gurus of the financial world,
including Robert Kiyosaki and Steve Siebold, about
this view that self-denial will make you rich. You
can't save your way to success, or starve your way to
proper nutrition. Kiyosaki, author of perennial best-
seller, *Rich Dad, Poor Dad,* agrees that the best way

to accumulate money is to earn more money. Siebold, author of *How Rich People Think,* notes that you aren't going to save your way there either, unless you're earning enough to have something meaningful left over that you can save.

A no-pain-no-gain philosophy makes people miserable. If you don't enjoy the journey, you're missing the meaning of life. Workaholics are famous for quipping, "There's plenty of time to sleep when you're dead!" It's cute, but misinformed. If your life is abbreviated and made more miserable by not getting enough rest, what have you gained?

Losing sleep makes you a loser.

SLEEP UNLOCKS THE POWER OF NOT-DOING

Mozart famously said that the pauses are more important than the notes. Jerry Brown put it this way: "Sometimes, inaction is the highest form of action." That Zen-like utterance early in his career earned Brown the derisive moniker, "Governor Moonbeam." Nevertheless he went on to have a stellar political career, returning to serve again as governor nearly three decades later. Brown accomplished many other things in between terms, including serving as mayor of Oakland, California and as state attorney general.

Sleep is a pause in every day, an interval that may be more important than the frantic notes we're banging out on our dull, out-of-tune instruments. Yet instead of being celebrated for the refreshment it provides, for the sharpness and clarity it lends to our waking moments, sleep and sleepers are shamed. Being tagged a "sleepyhead" when one is a kid is meant to goad us into taking action in our lives. The notion is that if we aren't harnessed early, often, and continuously to the grindstone of nonstop doing, then we'll amount to nothing. We'll be idlers, which is shameful in cultures that esteem "the work ethic" almost above everything else.

One of the more insightful classes I encountered in college was called the "Social and Intellectual History of the United States." Here we learned how the work ethic was tied to religious salvation in popular consciousness right at the beginning of American history. According to Calvinistic thinking, certain people were predestined by God for admittance to heaven. But what was everyone else to do? People needed the possibility of gaining admittance to heaven based on earthly deeds if life was to be anything other than a dour interval.

Thus, the concept of "a life of works" was hatched. This notion held that if you worked hard enough in this world then a spot might be opened up for you in the next. Of course, you'd have to pass through judgment and be deemed meritorious. In this way workaholism was positively sanctioned as the national obsession of the United States.

This work ethic seeped into Ben Franklin's aphorisms, such as "Early to bed and early to rise makes one healthy, wealthy, and wise." One of my favorites from Ben, promoting non-stop toil is, "Plow deep while sluggards sleep and you'll have enough corn to plant and to eat."

Having been a largely agrarian society, the work ethic was practical advice. The seasons wouldn't wait, so planting, cultivating, and harvesting all needed to be done on time, or you and your family might not eat. In this regard, the causal coupling of work-and-salvation made a virtue of necessity, which is a very functional concept. Why not feel noble about oneself? When there is something uplifting about doing what we must do, we can rejoice.

If working hard is a sign you are marked for paradise, then not working must be a sign you are doomed, correct? "Idle hands are the Devil's workshop." Thus if you sleep less, you'll have more time to work. With more time put into productive activity, you'll be more likely to be granted admission at the pearly gates.

Of course, there is a vanishing point. We can't work 24 hours a day, every day, can we? Everyone must sleep, whether it's a straight-8 hour stretch, or a series of catnaps, we need our shut-eye.

HOW MANY HOURS OF SLEEP DO YOU REALLY NEED?

We can debate how many hours are enough. There are folks that can get along on seven while others need nine. But the idea that we can gain an hour of productivity by shorting ourselves and hour is sleep is a myth.

According to authors Nagoski and Nagoski, we're net losers if we cut back on repose.

As they report, in their book, *Burnout: The Secret to Unlocking the Stress Cycle*:

> "It turns out that the physiological, cognitive, emotional and social benefits of spending a third of our lives unconscious outweigh even the costs in time, opportunity to do other things, and inattention to threats. Our whole body, including our brain, is working hard as we sleep, to accomplish life-preserving tasks that can best be achieved when we're not around to interfere. Quite simply, we are not complete without sleep."

It puts a smile on my face to see these authors saying, in so many words, "sleep-is-work."

I endorse their view, while observing that even they feel obligated to refute the socially frowned-upon notion that sleepers are idling away or wasting their time.

They go on to enumerate the benefits of sleep:

"We need it to recover from physical activity, healing and repairing our sinews and building muscles. We need sleep to complete the cycle of learning, activating our memories. Emotional catharsis is assisted, where in sleeping we can pummel our foes without incurring real world wrath and consequences."

The authors catalogue the ills, physical and psychological, that arise from inadequate sleep.

They conclude with the comparison that being up for 19 hours straight makes you as impaired in your functioning as being drunk!

THE FALSE ECONOMICS OF TRADING SLEEP FOR MONEY

I used think I was being super-efficient and cost effective when I commuted by plane from Los Angeles to San Francisco, to conduct a negotiation seminar that started at 9:00 AM at the University of California in Berkeley.

I live about 90 minutes away from Los Angeles airport, when there's zero traffic. I would awaken at 2:00 AM, start my trek around 3:00 and reach the parking lot at 4:30, catching the shuttle to the terminal. I'd check-in and pass through security in time for my 6:00 flight.

Assuming the plane arrived on time, I'd reach San Francisco airport at 7:15. I'd catch a cab to the city, getting to the seminar site at 7:55. Grabbing a coffee and sweet roll, I'd then dash to my classroom by 8:30 to greet attendees, pass out materials and notate a few vitals on the board.

After class ended at 5:30, I walked to the train to SFO for a 7:30 flight, arriving at LAX at 8:45. I'd get a shuttle to my car by 9:30 and arrive at my home around 11:00 or 11:15.

My day lasted from 2:00 AM until 11:30 that night: 22.5 hours! To say I was wrecked is an understatement.

After doing this drill about 10 times without any major problems, such as a delayed or canceled flight, my sponsor advanced the starting time to 8:30 AM from 9:00. This changed everything.

I adapted by not flying. Instead, I drove up the coast during the day before my session began. I got a hotel, and motored myself to the site the next morning. This meant I had to drive back home in the darkness, starting in San Francisco rush hour traffic, some 375 miles away.

I'd make the trip in about 6 hours, but I'd still get home at 11:30 at night, as I would when I flew.

In either routine there was no winning, from a physiological standpoint. I was slightly more alert for my class when I drove up the night before, but the regime was exhausting either way.

Finally, I started combining these trips with family mini-vacations. Occasionally, these involved tagging on another night or two for skiing in Lake Tahoe.

Since then I've declined doing numerous international seminars and speeches because they just don't make sense, either biologically or financially. For example, coming from Los Angeles, a one-day seminar in Asia requires at least a 5-day business week to deliver. Given time zone changes, it takes two days to fly in and be on site. Add another day for the event. And then it consumes about two days to return.

Your body is a mess from such a short turnaround.

Many sponsors would try to convince me they were paying only for one-day, the seminar date itself, which is a hoot. My counter is, if they want me for one day they'll have to pay for at least five.

At five days, I'm not factoring in the jetlag or recuperation time. The body needs to readjust from the time zone changes and loss of sleep sustained during the journey.

Add two more days for this biological recalibration.

And thus a supposed, one-day event realistically requires seven biological days to do. The price you pay is too high, even if you can sandwich in a day or two for tourism.

When you are job hunting and the position description says it entails "up to 50% travel," recognize what you're signing away in terms of health and happiness as well as income.

Harking back to my San Francisco trips, which took 22.5 hours or more to accomplish, that is almost 3 eight-hour days, right?

Let's just say I needed two days to work one day of seminar. Was I being paid twice my local rate? I was not.

Therefore, I sustained a loss the equivalent of one day's pay.

Let's consider that job listing requiring 50% travel. Are they going to pay you for your travel time and the overnight stays you'll need to do your job? What about compensating you for your recuperation time? Will they do that?

They may even try to skate on these expenses, forcing you to internalize them.

I haven't even addressed the toll this sort of work takes on you with regard to excessive stress. Simply interrupting, or elongating, or shortening your sleep cycles is disruptive.

Let's say there is a certain amount of "combat pay" configured into your compensation. Is it enough to defray your other costs?

ARE LAWYERS UNDERPAID?

Big law firms are famous for offering starting salaries to associates that can top $100,000 per year. That can be eye-popping to 24 or 25 year-olds, fresh out of school. And it can seem irresistible to those that are thinking of going to law school.

But, as countless disillusioned practitioners can attest, all that glitters is not gold. Seventy percent of practicing attorneys say they are unhappy in their careers.

To rack up the number of "billable hours" required earn their big pay, associates typically put in extra time, working 70–80 hours per week. Yes, they're paid double what an average occupation pays, but they work double the hours, under a huge amount of pressure.

The compact with the employer says if they do this long enough and successfully enough they'll make it to the perch of being a partner in the firm. They'll then participate in profit sharing and possibly their billable hours will be reduced while their hourly rate will increase.

But that's pie in the sky, bye and bye. It's not guaranteed, and given current "lawyer-nomics," it's becoming less and less likely.

Note the similarity here to with what we said about the history of the work ethic.

Strive long and hard, producing a life of works, and you'll reach paradise, right?

A form of this pact is present in almost every "deny-yourself-your-sleep" employment configuration.

I'm here to tell you it's a bad deal that is doomed to self-destruct. And the self it destructs will be yours!

There's no amount of money that is worth losing sleep over. And if you really want to grow rich, if you are currently incurring sleep denial, you're going about it the wrong way.

You need to be rich in sleep to be rich. In fact, if you are in sleep denial, if you are diminishing your sleep, you are impoverished in the worst way.

Let me give you an example.

I took on a challenging business consulting project. I learned a good deal, tried some new techniques out, and was paid reasonably well.

But the stress level was off the charts. I found myself having nightmares about the assignment, fretting about the impact I was having.

The tipoff that something was really off was the fact that I conked out early in the evening. I didn't have the time or patience to be with my children. I lived next to recreation, but had no interest in going outdoors or even having my curtains open.

I had just enough energy to work, come home, eat and sleep until I did it again.

Weekends didn't refresh me because I knew I had obligated myself to return. I dreaded Monday mornings and only got a sense of satisfaction from the paycheck. At the first opportunity, I had an honest chat with myself. I felt like a typical wage slave instead of an independent businessperson. After leaving this project, knowing I'd never come back, I instantly felt a surge of energy and wrote my next book in record time.

My sleep cycles returned to normal, which showed me just how out of whack they had become.

Once more, I appreciated the necessity of being the owner of my own body.

Above all, I realized how rich I am, right now, without a penny of extra money from an outfit like the one I had indentured myself to.

What I want you to realize is we are being conned incessantly. We are being talked out of our right to sleep and to prosper, right now, without anybody's permission.

Speaking of employment and job descriptions, there are companies that offer "unlimited snacks and a fully stocked kitchen" at the office.

Why would anyone need access to unlimited snacks?

Is it because of the fact that from lack of sleep, you don't have enough energy to get through the day without binging on carbohydrates? Also, let's consider that as you get fatter you're less likely to have the motivation to leave that company's employ.

You've become a wage slave, indeed.

Follow Your Own Personal Clock

We *are* the captains of our waking hours and of our sleep. Yet this secret is kept from us.

From the time we're old enough to receive rewards and punishments, we're being programmed to get onto other people's timetables.

They are the ones fixing dinner and putting it on the table. They start the classes in school at precisely the same hour and minute.

Our regimentation becomes internalized at a certain point, which is often referred to as adulthood.

"I won't always be there to pick up after you!" our moms warn. And sure enough, there comes a time when we have to gather our stuff, washing it and putting it away ourselves.

We learn to abide by our employers' clocks. It is they who usually say, "Your shift starts at eight and goes to five. You have 45 minutes for lunch."

Of course, these hours were an improvement over laboring conditions that existed during the industrial revolution. But now, we're losing those strides made by those that negotiated the 40-hour week.

With technology, work can be taken anywhere, practically speaking. Turning work off has never been more difficult.

For example, as a consultant I was asked to improve the performance of a sales team. The group was in continuous contact with each other. When one of them closed a deal, they had to report it to the others, regardless what time it was.

Their phones buzzed when deals were done and they, in turn, were conditioned to signal back, "Good job!" or "Way to go!" to show their supportiveness.

Even when they missed deals, when clients said no, or decisions were put off, they had to report in and share the disappointment. Inevitably, this meant you could be in the middle of your own sales presentation and be interrupted by the "failure" of another to get an order.

Mihaly Csikszentmihalyi wrote a fascinating book about peak performance—on the job, in sports, and everywhere, titled *Flow*. When we're flowing while doing something, time seems to go by without our awareness. We're so wrapped-up in our activity that things seem effortless and extremely gratifying.

Athletes have called this mood "being in the zone." Seemingly, in the "zone" they can do no wrong.

This wondrous state of mind first descended upon me when I was 12, as if from heaven.

Late for my Little League game, where I was slated for the first time in my nascent career to pitch, I stuck out my thumb at the intersection near my house to hitch a ride.

Instantly, a young chap in a red Corvette pulled up and asked if he could help. I said I was late and I had to pitch and he replied, "Buckle your seat belt." In a glorious blur, he got me to the ballpark in less than four minutes.

I had just enough time to make a few practice throws before striding to the mound.

What a game! I pitched from start to last. They scored four runs, which would have normally been enough to beat me.

But I was in the zone, so the script played out another way. We scored nine runs. I personally batted eight of them in with the three homers I hit. Our backup catcher was behind the plate that day, instead of me. He did a fine job.

But a week later, he broke his thumb, taking him out for the season. I'd never pitch another game in Little League, but in a way I didn't have to.

That one glorious day of flow, of being in the zone, created this fond memory that I'm sharing with you.

By the way, in regaling you with it, my fingers flew across the keyboard. Just recalling this magical afternoon put me right back in the zone again.

Those sales team interruptions I mentioned to you, with the constant messaging about sales made and missed, is exactly the type of modern madness that prevents us from entering and staying in a state of flow. We pay a big price when we permit these sorts of interruptions.

Imagine a babbling brook or a swift stream. It's a beautiful thing with its sights and sounds. Now dam it up every so many feet and it becomes a number of stagnant ponds.

These still waters invite algae, and the oxygen in this natural resource is diminished.

When we're flowing we're happy. When we're stuck, we're not.

Sleep provides a crucial opportunity to flow. But most people don't even consider it an activity. They wrongly think of it as inactivity.

The ancient Greek, Heraclitus knew otherwise when he observed:

"Even a soul submerged in sleep is hard at work and helps make something of the world."

There's that sleep-is-important-work idea, again!

Just as we undervalue the accomplishments of sleep, daydreaming is also derided. I would argue that it is restorative, just like sleep.

If we aren't permitted to space-out at least a little, our minds feel unduly fenced-in. Daydreaming allows us to wander off while awake. Sleeping and daydreaming can both produce a creative state of consciousness. Free from the demands of concentration, we are able to perceive connections between things that seem unrelated when fully awake.

For instance, many of my book titles come to me when I am relaxing, without a specific train of thought. It's almost a tickling feeling that comes over my brain when it plays with language and creates new catch phrases, mottos, and titles.

I'm not sure exactly what happens, but I know I'm flowing, or more aptly, my mind is flowing as these new notions percolate to the surface.

I can select environments that lend themselves to creating a new title. For instance, there is a particular coffee shop that is especially conducive. Typically, I only need a relaxed 20 minutes there until my awareness conjures something new, whether it is a title or a communication strategy.

I carry a clipboard, a pad and pens with me almost everywhere I go. Yesterday, when leaving the library, a title came to me as I was getting into my car in the parking lot. I stopped right away, pulled my out my pen and wrote down the phrase before it skipped away.

Nightmares Can Build Your Wealth

———∞———

Nightmares can serve as important financial wake-up calls.

I alluded to the time I was in Houston, Texas on a consulting assignment. More than anything, I wanted to succeed. The CEO was a genial but hard driving executive that brought me to Texas after he saw me deliver a seminar to his six-figure earning investment salespeople at his former company in Seattle.

One night in my Houston hotel I had a fitful sleep and awoke about 2 AM, drenched with "flop-sweat." Performers know what this is. It's the body telling you that you run the risk of falling on your face in the middle of your act, the body's way of expressing fear of failure. And it's anything but pleasant.

If you awaken with flop sweat, you can't go back to sleep. You're too agitated. The best thing to do is to address the thing that's causing you such acute anxiety.

I was concerned I wasn't going to have the impact on my trainees that I needed and specifically, I was afraid they would not perform the new customer service behaviors I was teaching.

My seminar would have been for naught. This failure would disappoint my sponsor, the CEO and would be a setback to my professional reputation. It would also ding my self-esteem.

After worrying for more than an hour, I set about devising a solution.

I asked myself: "How can I *make them* do it?"

Recalling my successful stint at Time-Life Books in sales management, I determined the only way to assure they'd implement the new techniques was to be joined at the hip with them.

That was it! I had to work one-on-one with each and every customer service rep.

There were a hundred of them! Even if I spent just half a day with each, coaching them one-on-one would take 10 solid weeks to accomplish.

This would require more funding and could seem to my sponsor and his management team that I was merely trying to line my pockets.

But I had to take the risk and tell them what I thought was required to get results.

Most training brought in by large companies suffers from the same flaw—implementation isn't built into it.

Many ideas transmitted in training programs sound peachy. Some can be brand new and very exciting, but they are not self-implementing. Without the right program design, the great majority of trainees will treat their training as if it is a buffet line, at most putting the sweets they like on their plates, while leaving the nutritious, good-for-them stuff behind.

If I'm walking through the line with them, or serving a fixed menu, I'm far more likely to leave them in a healthier, more productive state. They'll thank me later—maybe!

I explained this to the management team and they agreed to fund the one-on-one augmentation. It made all the difference!

We got amazing results and the program easily paid for itself many times over, as our performance measures attested.

I emerged from that project with a new and far more lucrative template for training and development, one where I could accurately predict and measure, and thus monetize improved results.

In short, that nightmare made me millions of dollars. I slept, in this case, not so well, and grew rich!

The stuff that keeps us up at night can be crucial to our success. Being well rested and restored from sleep is a desired and ideal outcome. But *not* achieving this result can be a critical indicator. Restlessness needs to be monitored and read correctly. It could be a needed wake-up call that you need to take action, to change something, or to not let something critical go unexamined.

How Productivity Is Misunderstood

I f we look at the roots of almost every time management book we'll find a tree that is delivering bad fruit.

That poisoned premise is "Do more in less time."

On the face of it, this seems like a great idea, doesn't it? After all, isn't that one of the essentials of productivity? If you get more done in the same or less time than the employee next to you, then you are more productive than she is.

That makes you a better worker and a better employee. You have greater value to the economic system because your outputs are of a lower cost than the more meager outputs of your associate.

Isn't that what it's all about? Do more and beat the next person, correct?

The overarching idea is that we're all in a state of perpetual competition and when push comes to shove, they'll be pushed out of the way while you'll be allowed to hum along at a faster pace. Until the next speedster, quicker than you, comes to the work floor and then you'll become endangered.

Like the weakest caribou in the herd, you'll be picked off by predators while your swifter peers will scurry on, unmolested.

Visit the gym often. Get into shape so when the thinning of the herd happens, either by outside predation or by insiders simply wanting to scare everyone into working harder and faster, you'll be saved.

The problem with this treadmill is no one makes it out alive. It is a race to the bottom, economically. If you're not a part of the ownership team, you'll be ground to bits in the machine that you're servicing.

And your wages, adjusted for the cost of living, are likely to stay the same or go down as new competitors are purposely arrayed against you in the form of cheaper and dumber labor or by smarter and cheaper machines and software.

Worse, along the way, you're building up anxieties and worry because you can sense, viscerally, that something is wrong, that the grim reaper will find you, that it's only a matter of time.

You're being set up to fail because it is a no-win situation for you.

This dog-eat-dog atmosphere carries over into your off-hours because your body and its rhythms are never turned off. Biologically, your job routine, including all the prep you need to execute it by grooming yourself and by commuting and by juggling a family are subservient to the official 40 hours that are being purchased from you.

Effectively, your work agreement governs your life, 24–7.

Peter Drucker was fond of saying you cannot simply get a "hired hand" to work for you because the entire person comes along with that appendage.

Likewise, you cannot dictate only the 40 hours someone is officially committed to laboring in your presence or under electronic surveillance of some kind. Their entire lives are bent, spindled and mutilated to deliver that quarter of their total weekly hours.

My point is this—if your job is too demanding, too stressful and fatiguing, physically, mentally or both, it is depriving you of the optimal enjoyment of your most important allotment of self-time, which is the 40-hour block we need for our sleep.

Today, as things stand in the United States and perhaps in much of the industrialized world, the work-block is at war with the sleep-block. If employers believe you can curtail your sleep block by 10 hours each week, and they can be donated those same 10 hours, they'll push you to cut back on your shut-eye.

This is obviously insane of them if you operate heavy equipment or drive a truck or have to pay close attention to your work. Sleeping six hours a night isn't the same as sleeping eight.

Accidents will increase, and productivity will decline. But if they can bully, cajole or con you into relinquishing your precious sleep, they'll secretly rejoice because they'll perceive they're profiting from your sacrifice.

Getting you to give up your sleep time is a victory to those on a power trip and sadly, these folks constitute the majority of workplace supervision and management.

There are lots of tricks they can employ to get you to work more and be paid less while sacrificing your repose. One of them is to give you assignments that require you to prepare for work or to do homework.

If you interview people for jobs, you'll need to read resumes and devise pertinent probes to discover if candidates might be a proper fit.

Let's say your first interview is scheduled for 7:45 in the morning.

When are you going to pore over that resume? Maybe you'll do it at 5:00 AM before you dress and get your family prepared for the day. That means setting your alarm for 4:30 AM.

Work officially ends for you at 5:00 PM but you don't arrive home until 7:00 PM after commuting. You would have to be in bed and asleep by 8:30 to get a full eight hours of sleep. Are you going to be able to shop for and prepare your evening meal and take the time to peacefully ingest it within an hour and a half?

Sleep researchers will tell you it is unwise to eat too close to bedtime. You're asking for a stomach upset and sleeplessness and even nightmares if the time your head hits the pillow is right after you've put down your fork.

Let's back-up. Instead of waking up at 4:30 you choose to peruse that resume before you go to bed. Is that as you watch TV or as you put food into mouth?

You see the challenge, don't you?

Work never ends, and sleep doesn't properly begin or last long enough to be refreshing.

You might number yourself among the millions that use a sleep aid such as a pill or alcohol. Scientists tell us these devices might induce sleep faster than Mother Nature, especially when you are feeling stressed.

But the type of sleep you're signing on for with these crutches is fitful and shallow. It isn't the dreaming, rapid-eye-movement or REM sleep so important to good sleep.

REM sleep is the most refreshing kind. It facilitates dreams, which are the repair mechanisms for our daily lives, enabling us to dissipate stress and enjoy fantastical sojourns.

Without deep sleep, we're grumpy and dissatisfied. We often awaken feeling as if we didn't really fall asleep.

Sleeping well is a "pay-me-now-or-pay-me-later" proposition. You cannot run on empty and have a fulfilling day when the sun rises.

If you short your sleep, or more to the point, if your employer is committing sleep-theft, you will pay a big price, in both the short-term and long-term.

Put another way, your bad sleep is making you poor. And if you allow it to persist, it will keep you in poverty.

You might be thinking, "Look, I pulled several all-nighters in college to finish term papers, and that didn't hurt me. I can miss some sleep and survive."

True, in the microcosm, losing a few winks won't kill you.

When I was traveling a lot for business I would occasionally have to take a night flight and try to sleep on the plane to hit the ground running upon arrival in the early morning.

It worked every now and then, but I couldn't do this two nights in a row and get away with it.

Humans are wired with what are called circadian rhythms. These are internal, biological clocks that predispose us, for instance, to being early birds or night owls. When we defy these pre-sets, working odd hours despite our individual biology, we can get out of sorts, grumpy, and worse.

If we're a morning person by nature, we shouldn't sign on to work the graveyard shift.

During college I did this, working at Safeway stocking shelves from midnight to nine in the morning. I'd hustle to catch a bus to college, taking day and evening classes, and somehow find time to crash in between.

It was an odd schedule and an odder life. When I was able to find more normal working hours, I adjusted easily and my grades rose as well.

Temporary emergencies and situations can be manageable. For most of us, the real issue is chronic sleep deprivation. It is especially pernicious because there is an abundance of secondary satisfactions to keep us in the dark about the costs associated with our sleep losses.

Sugary snacks, caffeine, and continuous diversions such as TV, radio, music and smart phones can distract us from what really counts. Like kids that don't want to hear it's bedtime, we block out our body signals telling us to unplug and permit our innate rhythms to take over.

Let me make an even bigger point here, an assertion that might really seem unusual and radical:

Work should not be our number one priority in life, especially if we want to feel rich and grow rich.

Our number one priority should be getting enough sleep and the right kind of sleep. This should become non-negotiable.

THE QUARTER-MILLION DOLLAR NAP

One of my best clients is a division of a Fortune 100 company. The funny thing about them is how we "met." They narrowly aced me out of another deal, before coming on board and hiring my firm.

So, having lost out to them, I wanted payback.

The best way of achieving that, at least in business, is to make a profit from your adversary.

Here's what happened. An airline was thinking of bringing me in to train its field sales force across the United States. It was a beautiful assignment, if I could snare it.

I would visit all of the major cities while doing what I do best, training people to be more effective in their jobs.

In this case, I had a leg up on the deal or so I thought, having completed a similar program, without all the travel, for the airline's customer service unit. In fact, that's why they called me to interview for the sales training gig.

I thought our get together and my proposal went well. I was optimistic until suddenly, the relationship went utterly slack.

My calls weren't returned. Time passed, and it became clear to me my bid was in trouble.

Finally, I spoke to the project captain and learned that a Fortune 500 company got the project.

But why?

At the time, they had a vaunted training division that was itself a profit center. Plus they asked an unusual question of the program's overseer.

It was a query I had never encountered up to that time, or since then. As a sales professional, I've always endorsed the idea that there is an answer for every customer objection.

But this was a showstopper. My competitor asked, "Goodman may be good, but what if he dies?"

Meaning, I was one-man band, more or less, so if we were in the middle of the training process and I became incapacitated, the program would be imperiled.

Later, I'd learn this was an insurable risk. I could have taken out a policy on my life that also protected against disability and business interruption, making my client the beneficiary in the event of my death or disablement.

But I wasn't given a chance, and the deal went to the X-Corporation.

So, I envisioned a future time when I'd make up for the loss by becoming X-Corporation's training consultant.

Happily, I got my shot, sooner than I thought.

A key marketing executive heard about me from a fellow employee in a different unit of their massive company. He had attended one of my seminars and sang my praises, which led to a meeting with the decision makers. I showed them a handful of my books, and made a proposal that packed a hefty profit for my firm. There was a little something extra packed into the proposal to make up for the deal they had previously beat me out of. Payback was within reach!

One thing I have come to appreciate in negotiations is that you need to downplay your interest.

If you seem too needy, you might end up negotiating against yourself, dropping your price without getting a parallel concession from the other side.

And if you're pitching a behemoth company, as I was, you'll make them nervous if you seem too anxious.

While I was waiting for their call, I propped up my feet on my antique roll-top desk, leaned back in my chair, and took a snooze.

The ringing phone awakened me, and it was the key executive reaching out to discuss my pricing.

Refreshed from my zzzzz's, I was in a very mellow mood indeed!

I spoke slowly with a calm tone and listened to his pitch for a discount.

I said I couldn't change the figure for the main contract, but if he wanted to purchase another 50 days of my time after that allotment was completed, I'd give him a 20% price break.

That did the trick.

To this day, I don't know where that idea came from, but it was creative, and it worked.

We did our deal, I was paid, and then we tacked on another 100 days. Fifty of them were at a discount, and fifty reverted to my standard pricing.

All in all, I estimate that little nap, consisting of a pleasant 25 minutes or so, netted me an extra $250,000.00, a quarter million dollars.

In other words, I was paid an added $10,000 per minute to snooze and compose myself.

You see, you can sleep and grow rich!

Sleeping has something extraordinary about it, a power to prevent us from doing something rash.

Simply put, sleeping is a great way to wait.

Sleep is a natural tranquilizer. It told my body and mind, there's nothing to worry about. Take care of yourself. Be calm. Let your stress go. If the deal doesn't happen today, it's not meant to be.

What would have been the likely outcome if I hadn't nodded off? My anxiety would have gotten the better of me.

Like most unseasoned negotiators I would have started to doubt whether my prices were too high. Did I need to discount before it was too late?

Maybe I should call him, just to assure him that I was still interested.

That would have been a bad move, signaling I really needed and wanted the deal and would eagerly "negotiate against myself," making one-sided concessions to save it.

Want to pay less? No problem, here's a discount on the whole package, start to finish. Reluctant to pay even that reduced fee? No worries, I'll cut some more.

Heck, I'll even pay YOU to allow me to improve your company!

If you can, sleep on offers before you respond. Take a well-rested timeout from negotiating. It can pay off handsomely.

By giving us the calm bearing of a confident winner, it can prevent us from impulsively grabbing inferior deals that can turn us into losers.

What You Should Know About Your Capital & Growing Rich

There's an old expression: *You'll never get rich working for other people.*

That's mostly true, even today.

In fairness, I must note there are CEOs of major companies that are getting rich through outsized salaries, bonuses and stock options, yet they work, technically, for others. However, they are relatively rare.

You get rich by deploying capital, yours and other people's. Let's start with yours.

Let's say you choose to drive for Lyft or Uber. You are providing a lot of capital to your joint enterprise. Your car, your insurance, your gasoline, your maintenance fees are all capital investments in your vehicle.

Your human capital, i.e. knowledge about the rules of the road and how to drive are also investments.

And there is an investment, actually an expense, that is something Uber and Lyft don't discuss much with prospective drivers. That is the aging, wear and tear, and depreciation of your vehicle.

By putting on an extra 1,000 to 1,500 or more miles a month, your vehicle will lose more value upon resale than it would when parked in your garage. If it is a nice, comfortable, late model car, this extra 12,000 to 18,000 miles a year could easily cost you $4,000 in actual cash value, every 12 months, or more.

If you're only netting $1,000 a month, you're giving away four months of capital each year for free.

Not to mention the wear and tear on you from fighting traffic and bending your schedule to be on-call at a moment's notice.

Now let's add your opportunity cost. This is the money and assorted other benefits and advancements you could be making at other places, working for non-Ubers and non-Lyfts that don't require your car-capital.

With these car service models and their breakneck scheduling, you won't be eating regular, balanced and well-chewed meals, and you won't be sleeping on a typical timetable.

These aspects of normalcy will be bent to accommodate customers like late evening bar crawlers that can barely spill themselves into your backseat after their revelries.

So, what's the good part? I can't say. There is no way to get rich driving for a living, unless you drive NASCAR and can beat everyone else on the track.

The minimum return on your money to remain in business is a breakeven return on your cost of capital, and it probably isn't going to happen with Lyft or Uber.

But they will make out because they have externalized most capital costs to you and to others like you.

Uber and Lyft are taxi companies without taxis, limousine companies without limos. In the same way, Airbnb is a hotel company without hotel rooms.

Capital idea of theirs, isn't it?

Or more to the point, it is a *how-to-avoid-investing-your-own-capital* idea. This is how some people get uber-rich.

The best tip one of your passengers could give you would be to warn you away from the ride hailing services if you truly want to make money, or prosper, however you wish to define this.

I have no personal gripe with these companies, though I am a little taken aback by their promises about earning extra money. As I pointed out, these earnings are nullified by your unaccounted-for costs, such as depreciation.

Essentially, I'm saying that all companies, especially these days, strive to be Ubers. They want income without capital risks, employees that are really independent contractors without paid benefits, and wealth without responsibilities.

If I walked up to you and asked, "Can I have some money?" you'd think of me as a panhandler, a ne'er-do-well or a parasite feeding on productive society.

Yet if that questioner is a businessperson or is incorporated, and asks, "Will you enrich me without enriching yourself?" We accept that offer each and every day and label it "gainful employment." Certainly we are being employed, as in being used. But is it gainful? Apart from their gain, I would say "No!"

Are we better off from our toil, more capable of earning, saving, and investing more money tomorrow? When you're stressing your way to a buck, wealth is invisible, or at least heavily cloaked during waking hours. And if you're toiling for no noticeable financial gain, you're only pushing wealth away. In these so-called "sharing" businesses, ride-sharing, car sharing, home sharing, we are actually paying for the privilege of whitewashing their fence! Let me explain. In Mark Twain's classic, *Huckleberry Finn*,

Tom Sawyer was ordered by his aunt to paint her fence. Being lazy, yet also ingenious, Sawyer conned his pals into thinking fence painting was an honor, and not everyone was qualified to do it.

Building it up this way, Tom enticed his buddies to paint Auntie's fence for him. Brazenly and without regret, he actually charged them for the privilege of doing this hard work.

This tale has become a huge allegory for me. I see it in so many areas of labor economics.

For example, let's look at today's book publishing world, where there is a widespread effort to make money without having most of the responsibilities publishers used to bear.

Chief among those duties is promoting the books they take on. This entailed securing publicity, getting book reviews, and courting chain booksellers and independent shops. Nowadays, effective promotion can often be accomplished mainly through pay-per-click and social media advertising.

In days gone by, publishers had works printed on actual paper with real ink. Today, having press runs is rare. If there is a paperback version it may be issued in a print-on-demand format. As each order comes in, it is printed and fulfilled on a custom basis.

This saves publishers from having to guess how many copies to produce while saving themselves from a reasonably large outlay to pay for advance printing. Publishers used to serve a number of critical functions. They selected certain titles for publication, and this required editorial know-how. They were important curators of content and gate-keepers. They also copyedited texts for errors and inconsistencies. They printed volumes, making sales estimates in the process. They put money into titles, by offering advance-against-royalties deals to authors. Then they'd invest more time and money in promoting titles through ads, publicity, book tours and channel sales to bookstores, large and small.

Today, because of eBooks, publishers can "choose" more titles than ever if they plan to eliminate or shortcut the other duties they performed. There is no practical limit to books they can feature on their lists because they will be made and sold electronically. With more titles being housed, by necessity each title will receive less editorial attention.

But most significantly, publishers are excusing themselves from paying advances to authors and from promoting the titles they take on. Publishers are Tom Sawyering, too.

Authors are asked to write their titles and to pitch them to publishing houses. They are then being required to promote their own titles, selling copies to speaking audiences, to social media contacts, and to corporations. Publishers are lending their prestige and really nothing substantially more to the mix.

In the next chapter I will share my secret for how the publishing world has increased my personal and professional capital.

A Test of True Wealth—
Are You Growing Richer
While You're Asleep?

You may be wondering why, in a book about sleeping and growing rich, I included a discussion about publishing in the previous chapter.

It relates to our topic because many ways of getting rich involve making money when you are asleep.

Every night, somewhere in the world, someone is listening to one of my audios or reading one of my books and I'm earning money from it.

This is *leverage,* one of the essential features of wealth creation.

For example, one title that I wrote over a four-week period is still spinning off royalty checks to me thirty-five years after it first appeared in print!

Recently, an executive who had read my book passed it along to his boss in Tacoma, Washington, who hired me for a consulting gig worth $80,000. During that project, while I was training his elite salespeople, the president of the division poked his head in and liked what he heard. He then hired me a year later when he became CEO of a mutual fund firm. That engagement brought in another $300,000, which eventually led to another million dollars' worth of consulting.

This wealth was all initiated by that one reader of my book. That's leverage!

It's akin to owning real estate that is appreciating in value, or income properties that are bringing you profitable rents.

How can *you* earn money and get rich while you're sleeping? This is the critical question you should be asking.

Can You Get Too Much Sleep?

———∞———

From Ben Franklin's wise words, "Eat not to dullness; drink not to elevation," we might infer that sleeping to dullness is no virtue.

But I still recommend trying it for a few reasons.

For one thing, as "Dirty Harry" said, a person must know his or her limitations. Humans don't come equipped with operating manuals that tell us to the dot how much sleep we need.

It takes trial and error to find out. As I mention elsewhere, because we're socialized to surrender our native, natural, individualistic sleep routines in deference to the collective, we may not know anything certain about our optimal sleep and waking rhythms.

I can tell you this about mine. If I get only five to six hours of sleep in an evening, I'll crave a nap after lunch. That nap may catch me up, even if it's an hour or two at the outside.

Add up the numbers and I need the typical eight hours of daily sleep to be functioning at a comfortable level.

They don't have to be bunched all together. Let's say somehow I manage to get nine straight hours, from 10 PM to 7 AM. Will I need a nap? Probably not.

If I get 10 hours, sleeping in until 8 AM, I could end up feeling groggy until noon. By that time, my head will clear. The grogginess is wasteful, of course. So, I'm paying a price by needlessly sacrificing an hour of my time, by feeling poorly, and by not being able to focus until I'm thinking properly.

I have found it does me no good if I awaken early and then try to stretch my sleep, fighting the impulse to get up and move around.

However, there are times when a too-much-is-better principle can apply. I do recommend pre-sleeping when you are facing a stressful event. Big events might include starting a new job, going in for a major surgery, appearing in divorce court, or preparing for a major speech to venture capitalists. When a lot is on the line, invest in pre-sleeping so you'll have a reserve of energy and tranquility from which to draw.

I confess I got too much sleep last night. I hit the sack around 11 PM and was awake by 6 AM. I got up, puttered around for an hour and then tried to cram in another hour of shut-eye, as I knew I was under-quota at seven hours.

I arose again around 8 AM, but whatever added sleep I got was accompanied by an annoyed attitude. I was peeved that I had to try so hard at getting those seven hours up to eight. It wasn't worth it. And it definitely made me grumpy, so much so that I was about to forego jogging at the beach and my channel swimming. The good news is that I talked myself back into my routine.

If frustrated sleep was going to affect me, why not sandwich in some productive exercise? I knew I wouldn't feel worse and I just might feel better.

It worked and I do feel better, which is why I'm writing this segment. I was struck by this observation—we expect perfect sleep, all the time! Society lays such a guilt number on us that we chastise ourselves if we don't get enough repose, get too much, or if it is of inferior quality.

I cooked some great protein the other night, seasoned perfectly, not too well done or too rare. Even rarer is the fact everyone in the family liked the way it came out.

So, I trekked back to the market to make next evening's meal an encore performance. I thought I did everything exactly the same way. But the filets turned out to be just so-so, and the former evening's raves were merely distant echoes.

Sleep is like this. One night it can be great, care-free, full, and lush. And the next, you could be tossing and turning.

Becoming perfectionists about what sleep should be puts an extra burden on us to perform. This leads to stress and guess what? That extra quantum of stress can keep you awake or make your sleep feel troubled. Sleep isn't work. But if we approach it the wrong way, we can turn it into work. Oversleep on occasion to determine your tolerances and preferences. The test of quality sleep is how you feel when you awaken. If you're feeling dull or dizzy or faintly headachy, these are symptoms of having gotten too much rest. If you're lethargic, maybe you got too little sleep.

BAD SLEEP CAN HIDE OTHER PROBLEMS

Sometimes we use sleep as an avoidance mechanism. We bury our heads under the covers as a way to procrastinate. If you're fighting against the idea of doing something while you are awake, sleep probably won't be a great tonic for what's ailing you.

Ask yourself, "What am I avoiding?"

It could be polishing or sending out your resume. Or you're putting off having "the talk" with your partner.

If you can take a single step toward solving the problem, then get out of bed, no matter what the clock says. I've found admitting to having an unsettled matter is a relief in itself. This small act signifies I am on the case; that I will get whatever is bothering me taken care of.

In another moment, I'll get drowsy and be able to quickly surrender to sleep, and that sleep will typically feel very refreshing because I have removed an emotional blockage.

William Blake famously said, "Excess is the road to the palace of wisdom."

How much sleep do you really need? Let your body tell you. It can give you vital feedback.

Purposely, oversleep and then see how you feel and what you accomplish the next day. If you feel great, do it again! In this way, oversleep will lead to the palace of appropriate sleep.

Not long ago, I did an intensive consulting program for a corporate client. It involved a nine to 10 hour day, five days a week, starting at 7 AM.

It was so stressful that I found my sleep was hugely affected. Literally, I was bringing home, and into my bedroom the unresolved challenges I faced at the job site.

This made me feel I was never off-duty, and this was exhausting.

I decided not to renew the agreement, allowing it to conclude at the initially agreed-upon time.

For the next few months I enjoyed the luxury of calm, deep, and long reposes. It was as if I was compensating myself for the foregone comforts the engagement required.

There is a key moment in the movie *The Bourne Identity*. A killer is stalking the protagonist. Bourne gets the upper hand, mortally wounding his foe in a field. Before expiring, the bad guy groans upon learning they work for the same employer.

"Look at what they make you give!"

That lament is universal. If you're giving up your sleep, you're giving up too much!

"Sleepless-Man" Isn't a Hero

L ike cheating death, many believe cheating sleep is somehow heroic.

They're among those that bellow, "There's plenty of time to sleep when you're dead!"

Ooh-rah! Ooh-rah! Ooh-rah!

These sleep cheaters are known to boast, "I get along perfectly well with only four or five hours a night!"

Maybe they do, in the short run. But then they crash. This is a fate they're less likely to highlight.

Why boast about sleeplessness? Isn't that just a little bizarre when you think about it?

I have this picture in my mind of these super-heroes in their spandex tights, with capes flying in the wind. And the "S" emblazoned on their uniform stands for Sleepless-Man and Sleepless-Woman!

What is their superpower? It is the power to stay awake when mere mortals nod off! In their estimation, sleep is weak, and it must be conquered or at least, be contained. Let's just consider the benefits of cheating sleep.

They can be grumpier, longer. They can shorten their tempers. They can abbreviate their attention spans. They're fitter to Twitter, nonstop.

I think if we ask these folks, they're likely to assert, "I'm a Type A personality!"

Recently, as a consultant, I had extensive interactions with an executive who laid claim to this moniker. It was a badge of achievement for him. He dashed around the building, poking his nose into every department, looking askance at those that didn't don serious faces and seem ultra-busy, as he did.

The funny thing is, he was incapable of growing his business. For all of his breakneck activities, at the end of the year, his bottom line barely budged from the year before.

Like the Nowhere Man in the Beatles movie, *Yellow Submarine*, he seemed to be scurrying about saying, "There's so much to do and so little time to do it!" Yet his efforts didn't provide traction, or the results he stated he was so devotedly seeking.

What's up with that?

I believe that entire premise he fostered, that he was a Type A, was a very dumb way to define oneself. What are Type A's all about? According to the literature, Type A's are competitive, time urgent, hostile and aggressive.

Type B's, to whom they are compared, are relaxed, patient, and easy going.

Which type do you think sleeps better at night?

If you're always fighting the clock, as the time urgent do, then you're likely to resent the sleep you must get in order to keep functioning. Moreover, and this has been shown, Type A's are stressed-out far more than Type B's.

If you can't turn off your working day, you'll ruminate, rehashing what did or didn't happen. This runaway mental activity is an enemy of regenerative sleep.

When I was consulting for that Type A guy, a curious thing happened to me. My sleep became more fitful. I dreamed about the assignment I was on.

When I awoke in the early morning, to prepare for the day ahead, I already felt drained and had an impending sense of dread. His Type A pushing was altering my waking/sleeping equilibrium.

This carried over into weekends. I felt sleep deprived and tried to catch up on the shut-eye I felt I had lost during the prior five days.

His influence was corrupting my rhythms and natural predisposition.

I've had enough occupational experiences in my life to recognize when I am being thrown off-kilter.

The *humanomics* of sleep deprivation simply don't pay off.

Let me explain.

For many moons my consulting practice took me far and wide for extended periods of time. An example is a program I did, training hundreds of individuals at a major financial company, located in Houston, Texas, and Kansas City, Missouri.

Over the course of eighteen months, I commuted every week to and from Houston. I left my house on Sunday afternoon and caught a 4 PM flight that got me to my hotel by 9:30 or 10 PM, Texas time.

On Friday afternoon, I caught a 3:30 or a 5 PM return flight to LA.

Although I had some down time on weekends that was really a fiction, as I never felt I was off the clock.

I made considerable money, and it didn't take that many weeks on the road to show me I was better off, as was my client, paying for an apartment by the month at the tony Four Seasons Hotel than staying in lesser digs. That way, I could leave five suits, multiple shirts and shoes and avoid the hassles of checking in and out, every few days.

During the course of that hugely successful assignment I was referred to an even larger financial firm that wanted to retain me. As I was already putting out 100% at the current assignment, I couldn't imagine accepting an additional client, as painful as it was turning away new business.

By the time we concluded the 18 month program, I was exhausted. All I wanted to do was return to LA and sleep.

My attitude can be summed up by Sun Tzu, who wrote in *The Art of War*, thousands of years ago:

"Victory with exhaustion means defeat in the battle to come."

I was victorious. I had developed unique productivity tools that I would later go on to share with and license to other non-competing companies.

These methods and the training programs I built to implement them brought in enough money so I could take off for months and even years at a time.

In truth, I had really created a *feast and famine cycle*, instead of developing deep wealth. I realized I wasn't sleeping well enough to become permanently and independently rich.

Burning the candle at both ends, as the expression puts it, is not a prescription for really making it as an entrepreneur, consultant, employee, professional, or manager.

Don't be fooled by those "work hard and play hard" come-ons that you see in employment postings. Explicitly, they're saying you can have things both ways, working long hours and playing long hours.

What they don't list among the job perks is the promise you can be sleeping well, too. They leave this part out of the equation because you won't be.

Put more stock in the expression, "If you can't get your job done in eight hours a day, you're doing something wrong."

In the end, your work/play/sleep "books" must balance. If there's too much "red ink" in any category, your process won't be sustainable. Your goal of getting rich and more importantly, of keeping the riches you get, will become more remote.

Don't conflate sleep deprivation with heroism. And don't let other people, especially your bosses or the Type A's, push you out of a comfort zone where you'll have to sacrifice your health or wealth by accepting troubled or erratic rest.

When you do the arithmetic of success, you must factor in all of the satisfactions you are trading for the dollars you are receiving.

True, I earned a great amount of money in a short calendar period at that mutual fund company. And I've repeated the consulting and training process, elsewhere.

But when you divide the dollars earned into the 24-hour days I was committing by being on site, and the recuperation time I required after each such engagement concluded, much of that apparent affluence is illusory.

Being cash-rich and sleep-poor simply won't co-exist.

At least, not for long.

IF YOU CAN'T GET YOUR JOB DONE IN 40 HOURS:

Over the course of my career wiser folks than I have shared some astonishing rules of the road and I'm happy to share them with you. The first one is,

"If you can't get your job done in 40 hours per week, something is wrong."

As I already noted, Elon Musk, founder of Tesla, Space X, and the Boring Company, is a widely revered figure in business. Certainly, he's a visionary and an innovator.

But when it comes being a role model for proper sleep habits, he's totally off the mark. Let's elaborate on his foolish habit of being Sleepless-man.

Musk boasted that he'll often crawl under his desk to get snippets of sleep here and there. He eschews conventional spans of shut-eye.

You might counter, "So what? He's getting a lot done, isn't he?"

Surely, he is. But he is also his own worst enemy.

I suspect his oddball waking and sleeping cycles have led him into making rash statements to the media.

At one point, he tweeted that he was taking Tesla "private," buying out its publicly traded stock.

He even asserted the financing for this bold move was already in place.

I don't think he was in his right mind when he made this announcement. By all reports, he wasn't taking Tesla private.

Second, there was no reported financing arranged for this purpose.

Third, the Securities & Exchange Commission came down on him hard for making such a claim. That purported disclosure seemed to be calculated to raise the stock price, which is a huge no-no.

And Musk should have known better than to have tweeted this out to the investing public, among others.

Yet it is the sort of rant that the sleepless are known for. Looking at Musk's purported sentiments before he uttered this misleading falsehood, he excoriated the "shorts."

These are investors that bet on Tesla's stock going down. Reportedly, Musk wanted to shuck them off, and a sudden rise in stock value would ruin their financial positions.

If you aren't on the emotional edge, you'll think twice before you tweet, especially if you are constantly in the public eye. You'll rein in your desire to lash out.

And you'll probably discuss with your director of communications what you're about to do.

The sleep-starved do the opposite. Like the over-caffeinated, they're likely to over-talk and say things they'll regret later.

Of course, I'm inferring Musk is trying to be a Superman or a Sleep-less Man, by taking his sleep in ounces instead of pounds. He's attempting to extend the working day, and to cram in far more than 40 hours of work per week.

We might be able to get away with this in the short term, but as a long-term habit, it's doomed to failure.

They say it takes a lifetime to build a reputation and merely a few seconds to ruin it.

This is exactly the risk that the under-rested incur by pushing the limits of their effectiveness.

Choose Long Term
Effectiveness Over
Short Term Efficiency

First let's discuss what the word effectiveness means, what it is and what it isn't.

According to management sage and my professor, Peter F. Drucker, there are several earmarks of the effective employee, manager, or entrepreneur.

For one thing, they know the difference between efficiency and effectiveness.

Efficiency is the process of doing things right, following the proper protocols, and avoiding errors.

For instance, I may do a quick, spiffy job of cleaning my desk, putting everything in its proper place, dusting the surface, and providing myself ample room in which to do my work.

In other words, I might be quite efficient at performing this task.

But as an executive, and an entrepreneur, cleaning my desk might actually make me ineffective.

Doing this task might be a form of procrastination. There could be far more pressing matters that I should attend to, such as making sales and marketing calls, setting up strategic alliances, and the like.

No matter how polished my desk gets, it won't dial the phone for me, or write the critical email, or make the outreach that is going to serve my purpose, right now.

In other words, cleaning my desk isn't the highest priority or the best use of my time. It's doing busy-work instead of proper business-building work.

Who cares if my desk is sloppy, providing I get done what is critical for me to do?

Anyone can polish this beautiful, antique roll-top. It doesn't require *my* attention. This task can be readily delegated to someone whose time is far less valuable. Only I can do other high-level functions and make the decisions I need to make.

Efficiency is doing things right, effectiveness is doing the right things.

There are even some things which simply should not be done at all. Even if you do a bang-up job with them, they are pursuits that will not help you move the needle in the direction toward furthering your genuine interests.

Let me share a funny story with you.

I applied to teach some business courses part-time at a local, private, for-profit college. My expert areas are in sales and marketing, customer service, communications, and entrepreneurship. I've taught these topics at UCLA, U.C. Berkeley and over 30 other universities.

Their human resources person called me and said, very enthusiastically, "We have a class for you to teach. It's Visual Basic."

I almost fell over. Computer Science is so far from my skill set, it's like asking me to perform brain surgery.

Could I have crammed to learn Visual Basic? Could I have taught it? There's a one percent chance I could have done so, under great duress. Even if I had managed to do it despite the pain, there would have been no future in it. The money was terrible, and the college carried none of the prestige of the other schools where I had taught.

No matter how efficiently I prepared to take on this challenge, it would have been the wrong challenge to take on.

Doing so would have made me incredibly ineffective.

I do a little bit of cooking for my busy family. I've come to enjoy it. We eat delicious, well-balanced and healthy meals, pretty much following a Mediterranean diet. I don't scrimp on the olive oil or butter, or freshly baked bread. Dipping the warm bread in the olive oil is a true treat.

Some of you may be wincing at that or at the fact I use a quarter-pound of real butter in our pound and a half pot of pasta. Yes, we could be more efficient in limiting calories if we used less olive oil and butter, and consumed less bread with our meals.

But if this came at the cost of making food so flavorless that we start to overeat or to search out less healthy alternatives, what good would that do?

I'm an effective chef, and making generally healthy and delicious meals, well balanced with olive oil and bread, furthers my family's goal for nourishing and satisfying meal times.

Moreover, I firmly believe if you're stressing about what you're eating, constantly counting calories while critiquing yourself for your lack of willpower, you're doing more damage to your health than the unhealthiest food might do. Thankfully, we eat healthy, well balanced meals, exercise regularly, and none of us has a weight problem, so I suspect my cooking philosophy is working out.

There is scientific evidence that says shorting oneself on sleep results in needless weight gain. If you aren't getting your work done in a 40-hour week, there is something wrong. Putting in far more hours than this will hurt your sleep and wealth-building capacity. You'll be grumpy and make impulsive decisions, as Musk did with his tweets. You'll also tend to rush through your meals, relying on processed items and fast foods instead of fresh. And because you're rushing, you'll gulp down your meals instead of savoring them, so you won't taste what you're eating, or stop before you're feeling full.

What's the good part in that?

Effective sleep habits lead to effective habits in living, setting the stage for your effective work-life and ultimate success.

There are no efficient short cuts here. Sleep cannot be delegated. You can't hire someone to rest and rejuvenate your body and mind.

Every day, when nature summons it, sleep is the highest and best use of your time.

Your Employer Is Not Your Sleep's Best Friend

Calculating how many hours you're at work is not simple by any means.

Let's say you are hired to do a 40 hour a week job. Then we can say you're at work for that number of hours, correct?

Not really.

For one thing most employers are required to give you a lunch break. By "give," please don't misconstrue that word.

They must allow a half-hour in many cases. A good number permit 45 minutes, and others one hour.

Let's say it's an hour. Sounds generous, but is it?

Not in the least, because generally you are not being paid for that time, if you're an hourly worker. You can't really go anywhere "off-campus" and get much done, other than grabbing some fast food.

So, from your point of view, that's a loss of one hour. If you arrive at 8 AM and leave at 5 PM it is nine hours you are committing to, not eight.

Most of us can't fall out of bed, rub our eyes, and be at the job site. Typically, you'll commute to your job, and before that you'll cleanup, get dressed, and gobble some breakfast.

That adds another hour and a half to merely get to your place of work. We were invested into the working day for nine hours; now it's up to 10 and a half.

If we add another hour to get home, that's 11.5 hours. But let's call it 12 because with some rush hours, everything takes longer and you may need to stop for gas.

That 8-hour day you signed-up for is suddenly 150% of 8 hours.

It's not a working day, and 40 hours per week. It's a working day and a half, or 60 hours, weekly.

But we cannot call the extra 20 hours overtime, because that is a term of art, entitling you to receive overtime pay.

Economists would label the fact you are donating your time, "internalizing" that time. It is costing you something, in foregoing choices to do other things, like sleeping an extra few hours per day, or going bowling, or bingeing on movies.

And your employers are making you take that loss, which economists label, "externalizing."

It is a condition of employment that you arrive there on time, looking reasonably clean and fresh, and nourished. Bosses thus externalize many of their costs of doing business onto you.

If they require you to "buy your own uniform," instead of providing one to you, they are externalizing. You feel and see the money leaving your pocket or debit card account as it is transferred to them.

Ouch!

It stings because your loss of money is obvious.

When employers rob you of your sleep, they are externalizing as well. Yet most of us don't calculate it as a loss, because it isn't as clear as something that we're paying for.

I am a student of employment ads, and I'm especially on my guard when it comes to companies that are going to externalize their costs, risks, and time-tables to me.

Today, especially among start-ups, you'll see ads that proclaim their business offers a "work hard, play hard" culture. Do you know what this means?

It means they're going to wear you down, chew you up, and spit you out. They'll insist on long hours of toil, and then there will be the after-work meetings, ping-pong blowouts, and watering hole soirees.

They'll even pay for the pizza!

You'll play hard, but not on your own, with the people you choose to recreate with, such as your family.

You'll play with THEM! And you WILL enjoy it and MAKE MERRY (said with sardonic emphasis.)

Some organizations state their intention to grind you to bits in fairly straightforward terms. Here is the exact language one company uses in its ads to tell you how it measures the working day:

WHATEVER IT TAKES ATTITUDE—This is not an 8 AM to 5 PM career. Our workday ends when all customers are taken care of. We must do whatever it takes to make our customers say "Wow!"

This company requires its sellers to check in and hit the road by 7:30 AM and their final in-home presentations to prospects may not finish until 10 PM.

Let's do the *arithmetic of sleep,* shall we?

If you're lucid and checking-in, dressed and ready to roll for an appointment at 7:30, you're up in the morning by 6 AM. If you didn't stop selling until 10:00 the night before, we expect you didn't nod off on the buyer's couch until 6:00 the next morning.

You drove home, maybe grabbed a snack, (not advisable for smooth sleep), and said a word or two to your mate or family. You didn't hit the sack until midnight, which means you were able to get all of six hours of sleep.

According to sleep research, that's not enough. By signing-up for this job, you're making a bargain with the insomnia devil.

Most jobs disguise the hidden hours you'll be required to log. Here is language that downplays the time commitment, also for a seller in the home services field:

Schedule: 8 AM–5 PM, Monday through Friday. Must be available evenings and weekends as necessary, especially during the peak Summer and Winter seasons.

This is simply not a 9–5 job if you want to see a paycheck, or if you want to see your customers when they have time to interact with you, which is after their own 8–5 jobs conclude. This job requires exactly the same time commitments as the one we discussed above. You'll need to check-in by 7:30, work until 9:00 or 10:00 at night, and weekends will actually be required, not merely "as necessary." I can tell you right now, they'll be required, at least 50% of the time.

Is there an alternative to this sleep-theft, to this externalizing of costs that employers are so fond of perpetrating?

There is, and I've exploited it.

For years, I've worked as a consultant on an independent contractor basis. This has allowed me to charge very differently for my time while pretty much dictating what is a "normal" working day and working week, for me.

Let me underscore how different this is from the 8–5 grind.

I was doing a contract for a division of a Fortune 500 company. Our engagement was going very well. My main contact, an enterprising and intellectually curious marketing manager, asked me what one of my other Fortune 500 clients was doing.

I said, "Why don't we fly out to Boston and I'll show you, if they're willing to host a visit."

They were, and we got a grand tour of the facilities and I showed off my techniques as they were being implemented.

After returning to Los Angeles, my travel companion was flummoxed by the fact that I had billed him at my standard consulting rate for the time we spent together on the flight out.

I explained that we were talking business, mostly, and the entire purpose of the trip was to edify him and benefit his company. He thought we were just palling around.

I didn't internalize the costs of that trip. I externalized them, billing him for my time, attention, expertise, and contacts.

I also billed the other client for my flight and for the time I spent consulting for them in Boston.

Without double billing, each client paid for something, and I optimized the value of my time, charging accordingly.

Along these lines, when I bring a "one-day" seminar to a corporation, I've learned to bill for it and perform it in a way that brings me a reasonable financial return on my time, efforts, and expertise.

Exactly, how long is a one-day seminar? Unless this is defined clearly, the phrasing can lead to conflicts. Companies could insist on the seminar starting at 7:00 in the morning, and going until 6:00 at night, meeting over an 11 hour span.

I often define it as 9:30 to 11:30 and 1:00 to 3:00. That's four hours of face-time, which some might refer to as a half-day. It is a full day from this standpoint.

I have to arrive on the scene by 8:30 or 8:45 to meet my contacts in management and set-up the room. People have questions and feedback to give after a program concludes, keeping me there until 3:30 or 4:00.

Then there's travel time to and from the site. Even a local seminar will require two hours in traffic. Plus there's prep time, to plan the seminar, customize it, and print handouts for participants.

When all is said and done, I may easily invest 12–20 hours in doing that "one-day" program. Although it looks like a quick four-hour gig to some!

You may have noted that I allowed for an hour and a half break between morning and afternoon segments of the program. Attendees appreciate the time because they can catch-up on some work and reach out to return an urgent phone call. It actually adds to productivity, and makes the commitment of human resources to the seminar something other than a total sacrificing of the working day.

Breaking at 3:00 serves the same purpose, enabling participants to get back to their posts.

As I mentioned in the flying example, as a consultant I can bill for my travel time, something that standard employees think is impossible to do.

It is impossible, if you fail to negotiate for it.

Which is a topic we'll turn to next: Negotiating your sleep time.

Let me emphasize the fact that your employer is not your sleep's best friend.

Which means you must be.

What Good Is It to Gain the World, But Lose Your Sleep?

———∞———

I t's 2:22 in the morning. My wife just woke me up. She can't sleep, again.

This happens because our neighbors have two old air conditioning condensers on their property. Located below our window, they make deep throbbing noises.

Though she's more sensitive than I, and she certainly has more acute hearing, I understand her complaint.

Our climate is what one air conditioning company calls, "Mediterranean." Even in July and August, evening temperatures rarely remain above a balmy 70–75 degrees, with little or no humidity to complain about.

Therefore, who needs air conditioning, anyway? When the mercury tops 90, which is extremely rare, we might run ours. Otherwise, it's about heating in the winter, which is silent to us and to neighbors because that unit is located in the attic.

Our neighbors seem to use their AC all the time. Outdoor temperature is irrelevant to them. Wasting electricity and having a bigger carbon stomp print are equally unimportant.

I've surmised they don't realize they can open a window, getting fresh ocean air in the process. Indoor air pollution is said to be about 4 times worse than outdoor, so they'd be doing themselves, the planet, and especially us, a favor to use a low-tech way of cooling their home.

They also don't realize they can put their climate control settings on the "fan" level and circulate their air without triggering their noisy air conditioning condensers.

My wife has asked them nicely, and insisted not so nicely in the middle of the night, to use their machines ahead of time. She asked them to turn on their system before 9:00 at night to cool their place, turning off the condensers by 11:00. Their home would be comfortable and she could sleep in peace.

It hasn't worked. Like rebellious children, or don't-fence-me-in renegades, they seem to take delight in letting the noise rip at all hours.

Of course, if she tries to gut it out without complaining, she is victimized by restless episodes throughout the night as the condensers turn on and off intermittently.

The next day, she's grumpy.

We have the right to the peaceful occupation of our premises, as do they. We shouldn't have to withstand a noise nuisance that could be abated. And they shouldn't have to be disturbed by their doorbell ringing with a complaining neighbor.

Once again, I walked her through our "remedies." They aren't pretty. All of them involve costs and risks.

We have a draconian homeowners association that enforces community rules. I'm reluctant to bring this issue to them because they are brutal, imposing fines on noncompliant residents. And what goes around comes around. Inevitably, we'll run afoul of the rules and our neighbors will complain about us.

Moreover, I'm not sure they are operating outside of their rights. We could use a decibel meter to find out if the noise we're suffering through is within a permissible range, per the homeowner's association. Ironically, they could complain about my wife's repeated complaints to them, asserting she's the nuisance. Our complaint could raise a ruckus, engendering more neighborly hostility, without doing any good to remedy the problem, and it could even backfire.

The same applies to suing the neighbor for imposing a "private nuisance." Using a reasonable person standard, the court could agree with the defendants that we are people of "extreme sensibilities," and our complaints stem from hypersensitivity with which the law does not sympathize.

The short of it is the possibility that we could invest time and money litigating this issue, and end up with even more hostile, defensive, and abusive neighbors.

If there is a bright side to all of this it is the fact that these neighbors are only occasional intruders, and not year round residents of our little paradise. So in a few months, if history repeats itself, they'll be back inland somewhere, occupying their primary haunt. Their rickety, old boat will be in dry dock, and all will be quiet once more. Still, we will have been through a needlessly sleepless summertime. The ultra-quiet of our scenic, unique, and refreshing lifestyle will have been interrupted. We have been *impoverished* by the noise, the hostility, and the torture of being repeatedly awakened by midnight machinery.

It is well known that persistently denying sleep, continuously waking up folks every few minutes, is a form of torture. It has been used in brainwashing and as a tool to force criminal confessions out of the innocent.

We may be in a paradise but it's a paradise lost.

To paraphrase a famous passage, what good is it for a person to gain the entire world, yet lose his sleep?

Not a dang thing, my wife would say. And I'd have to concur, because I'm the one that has to listen to and empathize with her not-unreasonable complaints.

For a while, before moving into this abode, we lived in a nearby port city. We had a delightful ocean view, with gently lapping waves visible from our living and dining areas and balcony.

But throughout the night we could hear the ding-ding-ding noises in the background, coming from the port. And we could spy the huge cranes as they toiled nonstop like the invading scaffolds in the sci-fi movie, *War of The Worlds*.

Everyone in our community could hear the noise, some more than others, depending on their proximity to it. Therefore, it was impersonal, and its existence actually made our oceanfront community more affordable for all. I once delivered a major speech on Little Palm Island, in Florida. Sharing the dais with a retired U.S. senator from that state, it was a neat event and a beautiful locale.

The sunrises and sunsets were ethereal, with hues of blue, orange, and pink. From behind my special sunglasses, at mid-day I could watch as the gulf waters changed colors.

Before we got into our cars and were ferried back to the mainland, my legs started itching something fierce. I mentioned it to someone who said, "Oh, it's the no see-ums."

"It's the what?" I asked with perplexity.

He explained that no see-ums are tiny pests that bite, so small that you can't see them, ergo their name.

Which made me philosophize about what Dostoyevsky wrote: "Man is in clover, but the clover isn't good enough!"

It's always something, right?

Now let's consider where to draw the line.

If your environment is keeping you up at night, or causing you the kind of concern that makes you lose sleep, it isn't worth it, no matter what the benefits are.

I just wish I could transform our neighbors into "no hear-ums."

Then I could enjoy the riches that are all around me.

Overcoming Sleep Problems

An astonishing number of people report problems with getting to sleep, sleeping soundly and deeply, and feeling refreshed upon awakening.

I'm not going to offer a cure-all, but there are some correlations everyone should be aware of that are preventing people from achieving the above.

If you eat heavily before setting sail for a snooze, it's likely your digestive system will be required to labor so much that this will prevent you from falling asleep or staying asleep.

Likewise, if you drink alcohol, you might put yourself "out" sooner, but you're likely to wake up prematurely and to have restless sleep.

Some people awaken frequently during the night to go to the bathroom. This is due to ingesting too many liquids before turning in, including water. Sometimes, physical infirmities, such as an infected or "weak" bladder, can be the culprit.

Others awaken, feeling their sleep has reached its fruition, yet only a few hours have passed. They actually feel somewhat refreshed, yet it's only two or three in the morning, and the alarm is set for six-thirty, presenting a lose-lose situation. They can remain under the covers, eyes wide open, staring into space. This is frustrating, and it's not unusual to start scaring yourself with hypochondria, by thinking you're ill, or worse. Now you've added anxiety to your sleeplessness, making it even harder to get back to sleep.

Instead of staying under the covers, you can check your email, turn on the TV, or try to distract yourself from the fact that you're losing sleep. Let me pause for a moment to highlight that word, "losing."

People hate to *lose* at anything, and the most competitive among us are always hyper-aware of losing—losing traction, losing ground, losing forward momentum.

If we awaken in the middle of the night and think, "I'm losing sleep!" we add to our discomfort and feel that we're wasting our time. This sense of loss is yet another stimulus that will make our consciousness work overtime and distract us from growing tired enough to seek repose.

There is a large body of research and literature concerning the experience of "loss," and its profound impact on our behavior and thinking. "Loss aversion" can be summed-up this way:

The pain we feel in losing a hundred dollars is far greater than the joy we get from gaining a hundred dollars.

As applied to our discussion of sleep, loss aversion means we bemoan lost sleep far more than we appreciate normal or bonus sleep. We grieve over it, which adds to our anxiety about whether we'll lose even more sleep tonight. The expression, "Don't lose any sleep over it!" sums-up the idea that sleep-loss is a serious outcome, one to be resolutely avoided.

I'm a body surfer, and I'd like to share this analogy with you. Falling asleep is exactly like riding a wave. First, let me tell you how novices miss wave after wave, growing increasingly frustrated in the process.

They eagerly swim out to waves, and then miss them, having to duck under water.

Now out of their depth, they can't walk along the bottom, and must use their flailing limbs for propulsion instead.

The key to catching wave after wave is to be properly positioned for them. You need to study exactly where they're forming, building, and ultimately breaking. Once you've done this reconnaissance, walk out to where they are breaking, calmly and steadily.

As you see the next wave forming, don't swim for it. This seems counter-intuitive, but bear with me.

The wave will come to you.

If it breaks prematurely, dive under it, seaward, so you won't be tussled. Then reset your positioning based on where that last one broke.

The goal is to fall toward the shore at exactly the moment it is starting its descent. It is the opposite of using effort and dissipating your energy.

The current has traveled thousands of miles, eventually resulting in the formation of this wave, and it has plenty of energy for you both.

Similarly, your body has plenty of momentum leading you toward sleep. Indeed, we even call the encounter with rest, "falling" asleep.

It is a surrendering, a letting go of tensions, a blending with a force that is incredibly powerful.

Just as it's pointless to fight with the waves, you'll lose in the same way fighting to get to sleep. Just as you're melding with the wave in body surfing, you're falling into your resting phase.

There is a crucial element in this analogy— *timing.*

If you're too early, you'll miss the wave as it washes after you. If you're too late, you'll also miss out as now you're in water that is too deep given where waves are forming.

There is a sweet spot, not too shallow and not too deep. And that's exactly when you need to catch your sleep.

Waves arrive in tight sets, consisting of three to six at any given time. Between sets, the water is relatively flat and there are no waves to catch.

Sleep seems to work the same way. Certain times are more propitious for drifting off than others. You can't summon waves like Poseidon, with his triton. You have to understand and not fret over the fact that sets happen, just as waves within them, also happen.

What techniques can you use during these flat seas? Swimming around isn't going to get you what you want, and the same pertains to sleeping. Just lying there fidgeting won't put you to sleep.

One of the techniques I use is to get out of bed when it becomes apparent simply lying there isn't going to make me sleepy.

I turn on my computer, which some say is a no-no. I read articles, books, and I also do some writing when I have a project of my own that will benefit from some attention. *However, and this is crucial, I try to do these things while standing-up.*

Standing transforms the process into a steady, almost unnoticeable form of exercise. As I'm reading, writing, or researching, I'm burning calories, a good thing, and I'm growing slowly fatigued.

My attention is no longer on sleeping. I'm accomplishing something, enjoying myself. Soon enough, usually after an hour or so, I'm ready to hit the pillows.

Usually this second-sleep is deeper and more gratifying than the first. I awaken at the appointed hour feeling very refreshed.

How long does that second sleep need to be? There is no hard and fast rule. If you have three hours before your accustomed get-up hour, then use them all. Even if you can only snare 45 minutes or an hour, I've found it's worth doing.

Escape from the binary thinking that says, "Either it's sleep, or nothing!"

There are alternatives.

Let's say you arise, go to the bathroom and now feel awake. Stand next to your bed until you're tired of standing. This may involve only ten or fifteen minutes, and there's no requirement for you to turn on your computer or to operate heavy equipment of any kind. Sooner or later, you'll tire, and your legs will be happy to buckle under the blankets.

This standing remedy can also be incremental. Start with standing in darkness next to the bed. Then, turn on the light, seeming to surrender to wakefulness.

Then do something. Make a list. Paint the kitchen.

Kidding!

You get the idea. Try it and tell me how it works for you.

While you're at it, let me know if my body surfing tip helps you to catch more waves!

HYPNOTIZE YOURSELF

You know how it is when you've adopted a new sleeping schedule.

At first, it's hard to adjust, but then, after a few repetitions of the new cycle, something uncanny occurs.

You no longer have to set your alarm. You start waking up slightly before it goes off.

Your unconscious has been trained, without deliberate effort or even awareness, to internalize the new clock.

That same power of the unconscious can be tamed for the purpose of leading you to slumber swiftly and without effort.

When I was a boy I wanted to stay up with the grown-ups, watching late night TV talk shows. The hosts seemed urbane, witty, and sophisticated, and my parents felt their IQs were improving.

But of course, late night wasn't right for me, in the sense that I needed my sleep as a kid and the school schedule forced me to get up on time.

"You should be in bed" my dad would nudge.

"I'm not tired."

"Yes, you are," he'd retort.

"I'm awake."

"No, you're over-tired Gary, and you just don't know it."

"Overtired?" Where did he come up with that whopper?

But his calm explanation had a somatic effect, and within a few minutes I could barely make it back to my bed, where I fell into a fast and deep sleep.

What I didn't realize was that he was hypnotizing me. By inventing a third category, overtired, he overcame the argumentative impasse between "tired" and "not tired."

I was so tired, he was contending, that I was unaware of it and nature would quickly spirit me away into deep repose.

This notion of overtiredness made me relinquish my binary negotiating position. I stopped asserting I was that I was not tired. I stopped resisting.

I believe we hypnotize ourselves one way or another. We tell ourselves one thing when we're facing insomnia.

It could be: "I can't get to sleep!"

There's a factual aspect to this. It is true; you're not sleeping at that moment.

But the idea, "I can't," introduces precisely what we don't want to contend with at that time: resistance.

"Can't" says, "No matter how hard I try, sleep won't be accomplished." The problem isn't in the not sleeping. One way or another, sleep will occur. As Mr. Miyagi told his young student, Daniel, in *The Karate Kid*, "There's no *try* in karate."

Likewise, there's no *trying* in sleeping. The exertion of effort will make you even more wakeful.

Famous martial artist, and later movie actor, Bruce Lee, explained the foolishness in trying when it comes to fighting.

We all want to be fast and powerful, he observed. Yet if we actively try, we are *efforting*. Extra, unneeded exertion slows down our strikes and kicks, and thus we lose power.

Lee explained that struggling to be fast and powerful launches opposing muscles into the process. One set of muscles is doing what we want, propelling our limbs toward the target. But other muscles are simultaneously pulling us away.

Here's another way to look at this. If you want to propel a rocket into space you need considerable thrust from the earth to just lift-off your vehicle. Gravity imposes a huge downward force on the rocket in its initial phase.

But once the craft leaves our atmosphere and enters the vacuum of space, resistance is lessened considerably, enabling a very small quantum of force to accelerate the capsule toward its target.

Imagine being able to initiate ignition in the highest part of earth's atmosphere, where gravitational forces are small. You could use less propellant, and go farther and faster.

Some missiles are being launched this way, from aircraft.

The point is, why would you introduce even more downward force on your rocket if you could actually lessen it?

Saying "I can't sleep" is doing this very thing. It is postulating the existence of a negative force, like gravity, that is standing in the way of propelling you into dreamland.

Instead of resisting, try substituting constructive autosuggestions into the process.

Tell yourself:

"I'm surrendering to sleep at the right time."
"I sleep very well, and awaken feeling well-rested."
"There's nothing to keep me awake."
"My body is feeling more and more relaxed."
"I deserve a nice, gentle rest."

When we say we can't sleep, we're also introducing an emotional overlay of frustration into the mix. We have a goal, sleep, and we're being prevented from reaching it.

We're blocked, and we despise the fact that any of our goals are being thwarted, especially by a phantom force.

This hateful feeling triggers aggressive hormones. Our bodies are being prepped for battle.

How can you fall asleep when you're standing guard at Fort You?

Aggression and relaxation are opposites.

We need a cessation of tensions, not an increase in them.

"But I just can't stop thinking about what X said to me, today!" you might reply.

If you're revisiting a struggle you had at work, conjuring up all kinds of clever barbs you could have but didn't hurl, you'll definitely sacrifice some sleep.

My suggestion is to say: "I'm going to deal with this tomorrow."

You can add, "There's nothing I can do about it now, anyway."

And say, "This will keep."

This is very similar to the advice I give to people with stage fright, whose anxieties start the moment they are told they're expected to give a speech or to talk at an important meeting.

I tell them to postpone their worries, to suspend their fears.

"I'll fret about this later. For now, I'm going to do Y, instead."

Here's what's fun about this practice—you keep postponing your fears until it's too late. You're being introduced or starting your talk, and by that point you've capitulated to the idea that you're going to be calm.

"Too late now!" is what you realize, with an inside smile.

It's the way I feel when I launch my body off my boat dock for a channel swim. My feet are already dangling in the bracing water, and I push off.

By the time I'm submerged, I'm already wet and cold and I need to move my limbs to generate warmth. Soon enough, I get used to the elements and begin to enjoy the aquatics. Another thing you can do is to put your worries on the clock.

"I'm going to give this 10 minutes more of my attention, and after that I'm letting it go."

You probably won't make it to a full ten before you relax, feeling slumber coming on.

The reason is that you have already begun to let go by the time you clock it. You've envisioned releasing the object of your anger, fear, or frustration.

I know a therapist who gives patients brief mantras that they are told to repeat.

Here's a very helpful one:

"I release, I release, I release . . ."

I've used it and it works very well with all kinds of issues. Releasing is the direct opposite of resisting.

You may have heard the wise saying:

That which we resist, persists.

First coined by psychologist C.G. Jung, this phrase perfectly describes the self-defeating nature of telling ourselves, "I *can't* sleep."

"I *can't* sleep" translates into, "I *won't* sleep" and "I'm *resisting* sleep."

Ah, but you shall sleep, and so will I, and so will most creatures on this planet because it is in our natures to sleep, regularly and refreshingly.

I release, I release, I release . . .

I accept the idea that I will sleep. It is inevitable. It's okay.

Nap-Friendly Workplaces

---∞---

Would you be attracted to a company that offered "a fully stocked kitchen" and "free snacks" over the course of the day?

I've seen quite a few employment ads boasting of these perks. I not only find them unattractive, to me, they are repelling.

This reaction is not from an aversion to fully stocked kitchens. I've said I do a decent amount of cooking at home, so I'm no stranger to gleaming counter tops, a well-stocked fridge, and other amenities.

I suspect that by "fully stocked," these employers are not inviting workers to roast turkeys with all the trimmings, whenever the whim strikes.

They probably have salt, pepper, coffee creamers, but nothing you could truly whip into a meal.

The "free snacks" part of the enticement seems beguiling, but is it? There are some diets that encourage grazing. They would have us eat four to six mini-meals a day, which to me seems excessive. I get along nicely with two major helpings and my morning coffee, supplemented by lots of cool water.

My problem with the kitchen and snacks concept is that it's really an inducement to stay on the job without taking a meaningful break from the action.

I sense "kitchen" and "snacks" are code words for slaving away in the coal mines without hope of breathing fresh air until the elevator brings you back to the surface after the last whistle blows.

If you think about it, constant snacking, along with sitting on our butts all day long, is a perfect prescription for obesity. This benefits no one, including employers who lose valuable working hours to fat-impacted ailments and diseases.

You might read this and guess that I'm going to prescribe the use of standing desks and on-site gyms. I'm not against them, but my thesis is more radical.

We shouldn't be deriving our bursts of energy from coffee, energy drinks, and sugary snacks.

We should be getting that second wind from taking a nap, smack in the middle of the working shift, if desired.

Workplaces should encourage and provide the facilities for catching 30–90 minutes of meaningful shut-eye, whenever employees need it.

Imagine being a truck driver who has just raced through the city, dropping off packages or other items. Between the traffic, double parking, darting drivers, and other stresses, he or she has been held to a tight schedule, really without a break.

Returning to the company's warehouse for the afternoon's load, wouldn't it make sense for that person to have a light lunch and a bit of a snooze? Imagine how calming this would be.

Moreover, by restoring drivers to full alertness, they would operate vehicles more safely, while lowering their blood pressure. Those packages would be delivered with smiles rather than snarls.

Insurance rates would likely drop, along with stress related absenteeism. It might seem that companies are donating an extra 30 or 45 minutes per day, they'd regain it in more effective and more efficient employees, higher productivity, and lower costs.

To American ears, this proposition seems radical and unprecedented. But it is neither.

Zappos, the online shoe retailer and a company known for pro-employee practices, has a sleep room in its Las Vegas location. Huffington Post, Nike, and NASA are also sleep-supportive organizations, providing at-work facilities for resting and napping.

Another example is Spain, a country with a long and storied experience with the siesta. This is attributable to sweltering summers when it made sense to take a rejuvenation break at mid-day, following a meal. However, the number of reported naps has fallen with increased modernity.

However, I can't help suspect an under-reporting of current-day siesta-takers, as there may be a growing stigma associated with "flaking out" in the middle of a working day, as there is in the United States.

Ardent nappers will be glad to share their bliss with you. Journalist and author Maya Kroth says her studies took her to Spain, where even in this modern era, she caught the habit. After leaving that land, she beamed that "I took my nap habit with me when I left Spain, and it's been my secret weapon against burnout and exhaustion ever since." When time allows she goes home to nap after having lunch, or finds a something suitable, napping in her car or at some other quiet spot.

In Japan, where people get the least amount of sleep at night among all industrialized countries, ad hoc napping is done practically anywhere. This includes dozing off at restaurants and even leaning against cement posts in the subway station.

Since practically everyone is operating under the same culturally sanctioned sleep deprivations, spontaneous napping in public is far more socially acceptable in Japan, than anywhere else in modern countries.

Part of the American prejudice against napping is based on the fact that infants and toddlers seem to do so much of it. Interpreting this as weakness and the absence of self-control, anti-napping authoritarians believe teenagers and grown-ups are getting away with something, slacking, giving less than their best, by seeking small snatches of repose.

They can't see any good coming from an activity that seems without apparent or immediate benefit to anyone other than the napper. Of course we know this is absurd.

Society definitely should have a positive outlook toward those who manage to become less drowsy, calm, focused, and energized.

For example, it is well known that surgeons make more operational errors later in the day than early in the morning. It is a definite social-good to have our surgeons performing at peak levels at all times.

Imagine having this conversation with a doctor who takes a mid-afternoon nap:

"You know, it's really infantile of you to insist on napping when you do. What are you, a baby?"

"On the contrary, I'm a responsible professional, and the life I save could be yours or your loved ones, because I insist on being well-rested and alert!"

That truck driver who stays alert instead of nodding off at the wheel averts catastrophe, as well. Is deciding to pull off the road to grab a needed nap a weakness or is it a strength?

Do societies, along with their employers, benefit from this act of accident prevention?

You bet we do!

In the United States, lost productivity from lack of sleep is pegged at $63 billion. While we cannot use any solitary statistic as ultimate evidence, in this case, I presume there is a far greater dollar-denominated loss than this.

And the human loss is unconscionable.

More lives are needlessly snuffed out on our highways by drowsy drivers than by drunk drivers.

Although I have no statistic I can offer about the number of workplace accidents that occur in large part because of tired, drowsy, or distracted workers, the number has to be in the tens of thousands annually, if not more.

The Manufacturing Safety Alliance of British Columbia has a lot to say about the dangers of workplace fatigue:

Studies indicate that the risk of making mistakes at work increases significantly if workers sleep for less than the average (7.5–8.5 hours) or are awake for more than 17 consecutive hours.

The effects of fatigue can reduce a worker's:

- Ability to make decisions
- Ability to do complex planning
- Communication skills
- Productivity and performance

- Attention
- Ability to handle stress
- Reaction time
- Ability to recall details
- Ability to respond to changes in surroundings or information provided

Fatigue can also result in:
- Inability to stay awake
- Increased forgetfulness
- Increased errors in judgment

Over the long term, fatigue can result in health effects, such as loss of appetite and digestive problems, and other chronic health conditions, including depression.

These effects can result in:
- Increased sick time, absenteeism, and rate of turnover
- Increased medical costs.

One study has shown that fatigue can have similar effects to drinking alcohol:
- 17 hours awake is equivalent to a blood alcohol content of 0.05 (the legal limit in British Columbia).
- 21 hours awake is equivalent to a blood alcohol content of 0.08

- 24–25 hours awake is equivalent to a blood alcohol content of 0.10

Two important things employers can provide are:
- On-site accommodations, and
- Facilities where workers can nap either during the shift or before driving home.

I began this section by citing two of the perks being touted in today's job postings—snacks and a fully stocked kitchen.

There is a third perk we often see mentioned. Many employers are quick to offer a "great work/life balance." Some deliver slightly on this promise.

This can take many forms, though most employers seem to leave this benefit undefined. *Flex-time* comes to mind as a plus, enabling folks to schedule important life events with ease, such as dentist appointments, picking up and dropping off of kids, and time away to attend graduations and weddings.

What few point to or offer in any way is a meaningful Work + Sleep Balance. Several years ago, then trendy advertising agency Chiat/Day reportedly hung a poster in their offices:

"If You Don't Come In On Saturday, Don't Bother Coming In On Sunday!"

This, of course, is not what I mean. Any culture that celebrates sacrificing shut-eye and the inhuman hours its employees rack-up, is the opposite of one that has a proper work/life balance.

It's simply impossible to enjoy your life when you're chronically tired. As I've shown, it is also unsafe for you and for others.

It is also impossible to generate sizable wealth for yourself in the process, or for your employer.

You're Awake, You're Alive & You Feel Fantastic!

—— ⧖ ——

Obviously, sleeping is wonderful. It is restorative and restful.

The moment you awaken, however, is an even greater occasion. Here is the real opportunity. We get a chance to greet the day; to set the stage for prosperity.

Just like the saying—you only have one chance to make a good impression—the same can be said about rousing yourself from slumber. You get one chance to do it right; to poise yourself for success.

I'm going to share with you several ways to do this.

Inspirational speaker Esther Hicks proposes that we meet the day with thanks.

Say thank-you for another chance to do well, to succeed, and to be happy. You've just hit the reset button on your life and this day is a clean slate.

Pausing to appreciate where you are, what you have, the people in your life, and the people not in your life, your specific abilities and challenges. All of this is empowering.

We don't have to succumb to the negative habit of wishing we had gotten more sleep or disparaging what is to come. Just lie there, eyes opened or shut or somewhere in-between.

Then say, "Thank you," aloud or silently. By doing this you've launched the day in a way that will bring you even more for which to be grateful.

I like a phrase shared by one of my employees. She, in turn, heard it somewhere else, making it impossible for me to give its author full credit.

Upon achieving consciousness say, "I'm Awake, I'm Alive, and I Feel FANTASTIC!"

You won't miss the irony in this statement if you're hung over from too much partying or working the night before. It can even bring a smile to your face because of the possibly huge disconnection between your aches and pains and your spoken sentiments.

This is good because laughing at yourself and your situation will lighten you up, which is partly the aim of these affirmations.

The late Zig Ziglar, one of my favorite self-improvement authors, advocated doing something other than awakening and simply rising. Anyone can do that, and most do, without enthusiasm.

He said our goal is to quickly move from grump-iness or indifference into energized positivity. It is only from becoming aggressively enthusiastic that we'll be able to succeed.

So, his tonic is to wake up, put your feet on the floor, and start clapping your hands!

It sounds outrageous, doesn't it?

But harken back to that nursery school song, "If you're happy and you know it clap your hands!"

As kids, we loved doing it. So why not do it as grown-up kids?

I can tell you from personal experience that it works. As a professional speaker on the road, wak-ing up in hotel rooms, I found again and again that ignoring my jet lag and applauding perfectly sets the stage for a wonderful day.

Within hours, I usually hear that applause com-ing back to me from grateful audiences, because I earnestly shared information with them, instead of drolly rolling it out.

Clapping and other techniques succeed, in spite of our feelings that they are goofy. As Dale Carnegie shared:

"If you act enthusiastic, you'll BE enthusiastic."

This is an incredible behavioral phenomenon, sometimes called the "act-as-if" principle.

Taking on the outer appearance of a positive emotion tends to make it manifest inside of us.

William James, an early psychologist, posed the same theory, proposing it as a question:

"Do we run because we're afraid, or are we afraid because we run?"

The answer is, "both."

We can actually make you feel the emotion of fear or anxiety if you'll follow this simple direction.

Begin to breathe shallowly. Speed it up, so you're panting. Within 30 seconds, and probably no more, you'll begin to grow concerned about your health or well-being, guaranteed!

Please remember, we're doing this only to demonstrate a point!

We associate being out of breath with being out of control and as creatures we don't like this out of control feeling. It distresses us.

Even though you know that I induced you to do this exercise, by following my direction, your body will send a signal to your brain that something is wrong, though you know nothing is at all the matter. Deep in the reptilian part of our being, we reject this explanation, succumbing instead to emotions that are more primal. You can stop feeling anxious or fearful in a second when you restore regular breathing.

Happily, the same principle applies to tricking ourselves into feeling enthusiastic and optimistic.

We don't clap without a good reason. Although we've artificially begun this act, thinking it silly and unbecoming, as we continue doing it something else takes over.

Like priming a pump, we're "wasting" a little water to make the real thing gush out in quantity.

Our positive emotions flow forth because we associate clapping with appreciation, with having been rewarded, with liking something and wanting to get more of it.

You've had a terrible night's sleep. So, what?

Say "thank you," repeating it often.

Tell yourself, "I'm awake, I'm alive, and I feel fantastic!"

Start clapping, and don't stop until you're enthused and a grin is on your face.

I like reciting this affirmation, first thing in the morning: "I'm rich!"

This is especially useful when I'm feeling anything but affluent.

Maybe I had an expensive car repair as I did the other day. Unexpectedly, when taking a break from recording one of my books in a Hollywood studio, my car simply stopped running in the middle of the street.

It didn't help matters that the temperature was over 100 degrees! I phoned the auto club and they asked, "Are you in a safe place?"

"No!" I shouted back over the din of passing traffic and honking horns.

Cars were barely stopping behind me, ignoring my hazard lights and waving arm, telling them to go around me.

The tow truck took me to the nearest Mercedes dealership.

"My gosh, this is going to cost a ton!" I recall thinking. I typically use local, independent repair shops.

I was feeling exhausted, impoverished, and almost overwhelmed because I still had half or more of the book to record. At first, they informed me it was going to be a small repair. Then they came back and broke the bad news.

After that small repair, my car still wasn't running. I needed a new fuel pump.

But not to worry—I'd be loaned a brand new Mercedes courtesy car that would enable me to drive the 55 miles back to my home, return the next day, finish recording, and then pick-up my regular ride.

It turned out they needed an extra day to finish the repair.

Somewhere in the middle of this chaos I started to relax.

I let go of my concern about the repair expense. I began to enjoy the free coffee and refreshing air conditioning in the dealership. I wasn't sitting in traffic, risking being rear-ended and stressed.

I recognized that I was getting the velvet glove treatment, really communicative customer service, which I appreciate.

At last, I started feeling rich, instead of poor.

Suddenly, I saw all of the positives in the experience. First, I stalled in the middle of civilization, not in a remote, deserted location. It was a weekday.

Though I had pushed to do the recording on a Saturday, the studio declined. Now I was relieved the car stalled out during the workweek when dealers were actually open.

I was even glad an authorized dealer was in charge of the repair. That gave me confidence the job would be done right.

A zillion things went perfectly, including the book recording, which I believe is one of my best. In spite of this sorry episode, I still completed the job in the anticipated amount of time.

My voice didn't reveal any agitation on any of the sound tracks.

What was it, exactly, that turned things around?

It was that simple affirmation: "I'm rich."

What is a slightly inconvenient and even rather costly repair to someone who is rich?

It's a mere blip on the screen and nothing to stay agitated about.

When you start your day with this maxim, repeating to yourself, "I'm rich," your experience will show you the many ways in which you are wealthy.

I left that episode with an added insight. My car is a classic. I love it. When I retrieved it at the dealer's, it was gleaming from having been freshly detailed.

After test-driving that loaner I can honestly enthuse that my car rides better than the new ones, and it is far more sporty and beautiful.

When I drive it I feel truly rich.

I'm not missing a thing by watching the newer models being shown at the dealership.

I hope current buyers feel the way I do, after 10 or 11 years have passed.

You are rich, too.

Start the day wonderfully by reminding yourself of this fact.

Getting Inside the Blissful Sleep Bubble

In the TV show and movie, *Get Smart,* a "cone of silence" descends, surrounding the protagonists. This bubble enables them to have a spontaneous, confidential conversation.

That zone of impermeability, like two coats of armor, is something everyone should have in their arsenal to fend off everyday distractions and subtractions.

My dad had this bubble, which I envied for many years. It wasn't a cone or chain mail but it was an unshakable aura of calmness and tranquility. He simply wouldn't let negativity get him down or even a series of unfortunate events tarnish his sheen.

I asked him once or twice how he could maintain his composure, when I'd have been freaking out.

"If something bothers you, just cut it out of your mind."

And with a type of karate chop, he made the two-part motion of doing this, starting at his forehead, and finishing his motion with his "bladed" hand moving away at a right angle from his shoulder.

I thought it was hokey, and dumbly metaphysical. I've come to learn, having a number of my own, that kids can be literalists.

They'll say, "You can't get into your mind and cut something out with the magical sweeping of your hand. That's preposterous."

That *was* my opinion. And I felt pretty much the same way about his musings about maintaining a positive mental attitude.

"It's just as easy to think positively as it is negatively, Gary."

Wrong again, Dad.

If something bothered me it wasn't going to stop bothering me just because I wanted it to.

Like the time I was nine years old and playing municipal league baseball. We lost a playoff game by the score of one to nothing.

I made the last out, which felt catastrophic. My family had plans to eat at our favorite restaurant near the ball field. And I couldn't stop my tears of shame from flowing.

"It's all right Gary. Eliot pitched a PERFECT GAME! Nobody got on base! Nobody got a hit! You'll get over it."

No, no, no, I wasn't getting over THIS. "I could have tied the game with one swing," I kept ruminating.

And of course, as I write this you can tell the memory is as fresh as it could be. I'm back at bat, swinging and missing. Then I'm ignoring my food, which would never taste as good as it once had.

Tell me how you cut this type of episode out of your mind.

In spite of my protests, Dad could remain calm in the worst tempests. I admired that, and still do.

How could he pull this off?

He didn't drink. He didn't take tranquilizers. He didn't binge on ice cream or desserts.

I believe I have finally cracked the code, and I'm happy to share it here with you.

Dad slept as long as he liked. Usually, he was still in bed, snoozing away blissfully, when most grown-ups were commuting to work or had already arrived.

This was simply a fundamental fact of his existence. Dad's sleep was non-negotiable.

Looking back, I understand why he didn't practice law. That would have involved early mornings, having to adhere to courtroom calendars, being pinned to a schedule not of his making.

He elected to be a "glamorous" salesperson. Titles varied. In some circumstances he was an Account Executive and in others a Senior Vice President.

But always, his forté was rainmaking, bringing in the business to whatever enterprise that cut his checks.

This meant he could set his own meeting times, and he would always elect to have the first no earlier than at 11:30 in the morning. Typically, even this time was a push for him, so he'd drop in on his business prospects around 1:30 in the afternoon, and then occasionally meet a second one at 3:30.

As I've detailed in my book, *How To Sell Like a Natural Born Salesperson*, my father's closing ratios were high, callbacks were few, and paperwork was minimal.

Following *his* father's advice, my parent learned to keep his business "under his hat."

He never allowed junior sellers to shadow him, and he actively avoided becoming a sales manager where he would be expected to mentor others, thus revealing his trade secrets.

He made a point of making his calls from home to set appointments, which endowed him with a shroud of mystery, not totally unlike that cone of silence we talked about.

Long before books touted the idea of the 80/20 rule, focusing on the important few instead of the trivial many actions one could take, he was doing this. He was always conserving and then directing his focus, like a laser.

You may have heard the adage, propagated in classical sales movies like *Glengarry Glen Ross,* that top sellers do their ABCs. Always-Be-Closing is their mantra.

Many approach this concept by staying hyper-busy, asking irrelevant and powerless people to buy, and then pestering them with follow-ups.

This type of overkill was anathema to my father. He didn't aim a scattergun. He used a rifle shot and was to selling what a marksman is to target shooting.

If dad had a secret motto, it could have been: *Always Be Sleeping*!

Preserving your energy is the highest priority, then deploying it. But to do this effectively, you need to regularly replenish it.

That utter calmness, I now know, really came from recharging his batteries regularly, while others drew on them incessantly, which slowed them down and made them stall.

Dad never tried to be a machine, or to emulate one in any way.

I've noted before that I follow employment ads very carefully. They are a window into the work styles and thinking of today's companies.

I especially love to deconstruct sales job ads, to get a sense of what "a day in the life" is at various places of business. When I see ads that say, "You'll make 150 calls a day," I simply laugh out loud.

If you're calling from business to business, even using an auto-dialer, it's going to be very difficult to reach anywhere near this number of "live" contacts.

The entire premise of the job is off-kilter. If your prospecting necessitates panning tons of silt every day just to find a few microscopic nuggets of gold, you'll go broke.

The only way to accomplish this is by turning yourself into a machine, and good luck with that. We might be able to do repetitive tasks for a while, but we're bound to burn out. This has been known in assembly line work forever. Repetitive motion disorders vex you physically, and you can't help yourself from spacing out, which is also dangerous.

The dream of most employers, whether they admit it or even consciously are aware of it, is to have zero-cost laborers that require zero maintenance and zero down time.

They don't exist, even in robotic form. Robots need to be greased, maintained, repaired, and ultimately upgraded and replaced.

Humans are worse! We make terrible machines.

The downtime we need, every single night is that which is dedicated to sleep.

Do your own preventive maintenance. Make sure not to bargain away your allotment of downtime.

And let me say this. Even if you are in the pluck of youth, you can only compromise your sleep time in the short run before you break down.

When I was taking a full-time load of units in college, I was also responsible for running a business office across a 12-hour day, from 9 to 9. Plus, I had to oversee a shorter 4-hour shift on Saturdays, during which I'd supervise salespeople and do the weekly payroll.

I went to my doctor with a cold. He took my blood pressure and asked me point blank: "Tell me how a 19-year old can have high blood pressure?"

I began to describe my extended day, the management job I held down, and the classes I took.

He only let me get so far before he cut me off with a wave of his hand.

"Enough!" he said. "I understand now."

What I'm saying again is this sleep advice isn't only pertinent to advanced adults, as my dad was when I observed his sleep style.

I'm talking to *you*, whoever you are!

You may feel you're getting away with something, but sleep deprivation will catch-up with you.

My point in this chapter really pertains to calmness, to maintaining the sort of admirable and enviable tranquility that my dad had.

I now know how to get there.

I was there, yesterday. My wife asked me, "How can you be so calm?"

We are facing a few minor challenges and deadlines, and she was right. I was especially at ease in the midst of the crosswinds.

Finally, and I mean this for the first time in my life, I felt to my bones the tranquility my father had possessed.

Free from worry and anxiety, my body felt healthy and rested, my mind was clear, and I was simply contented.

Nothing was missing and nothing could be added.

She saw and immediately registered what I felt. It was that palpable and unmistakable.

When I was a kid I saw my dad's calmness as if he was in a bubble and I was outside, looking in. Now I was in that bubble.

It felt great.

I realize now that an essential precursor to achieving this bliss is getting as much rest as you personally need and desire.

Dad knew, and now you and I know, as well.

Sleepless? Don't Try

There are a zillion hacks for beating sleepless-ness. Drugs and counting sheep are just two of them.

My take on this is a little different.

For one thing, and this is the main thing, you're simply not tired enough to drift off into blissful slumber.

Yesterday, leaving our kids to their homework, my wife and I set off to visit a museum we frequent, usually with them in tow. This sojourn introduced its own stresses and satisfactions.

Would we have enough to talk about, just the two of us? That notion made our trek feel like a first date.

Would we only talk about our kids, thus dimin-ishing the "date-ness" of the escapade?

We had a nice drive in. Sadly, an uninspired docent guided our tour. She had her pick of the "highlights" of the collection and yet she chose the most uninspiring pieces to share.

Adding to the disappointment, when she asked for our input, my wife offered hers, which was a brilliant comment, but shunned by she who asked for it.

This induced my lovely to whisper, "Let's ditch the tour," which we did, forthwith.

On the drive home we stopped to buy some specialty foods at a store we don't have in our neighborhood. I had to deftly evade a runaway bunny on the freeway, and then we went to the beach, adding our kids for the occasion.

I jogged and they surfed.

By the time we made dinner, around 6:00, I was tired enough to hit the sack. I was seriously bushwhacked, between the tensions of the outing and the powerful headwinds I fought as my feet pounded the chilly autumnal sand. I mentioned this to my wife, whose drooping eyelids fluttered in agreement. She was spent, too. Of course, 6 PM was too early to retire as sleeping in mid-evening portended middle of the night insomnia. So, I waited until 9:00, and I had no problem drifting away.

I awoke around 2 AM for a half hour, did some reading, and went back to bed until 8:00.

Yep, that means I got about 11 hours of shut-eye.

I said I was tired!

And this is the point. Wear yourself out. Take a long ride. Visit a museum. Then hit the waves or the sand.

This was my prescription for exhaustion, and of course, you don't have to replicate it, jot for jot.

But there are things *you* can do that match this list of activities. But note that word, activities.

When we reduce it to a single term, we were *active!*

We got out. There was tension, drama, physical activity, between driving and seeing the passing landscapes, and walking around the cavernous museum buildings.

The topper was the ocean visit, which by itself would have taken a pleasant toll. But that, added to everything else, and making and serving dinner did us in.

Trying to sleep when you're not tired is a big mistake. Yet it is something people do all the time.

Erroneously, we believe we can turn off our consciousness the same way we turn off a bedside lamp. One click or snap of the fingers and we're out like a light, but clearly sleep doesn't work on command.

We don't command it. It commands us.

When we're tired enough, it overwhelms us.

One sign that sleep is stalking me is when my eyes tear-up for no reason. They water so much that I have to wipe away the excess moisture.

"You want to stay awake?" the Sleep Monster mocks. "Then try doing it with blurry eyes that refuse to clear!"

At that point, it's simply easier to succumb than to resist.

And what happens after that? What sort of sleep do I experience?

Well, it's usually blackout sleep. Dreamless until awakening, I'm dead to the world for a long, uninterrupted span.

It's also refreshing.

Let me repeat what Mr. Miyagi admonished his young protégé in the movie, *Karate Kid*, "There is no 'try' in karate."

You can't force it. What Miyagi didn't explain is the fact that when we try too hard to do anything, we set into motion opposing forces. These create the equivalent of friction.

Bruce Lee noticed when most new martial artists want to punch faster, they "muscle-it," pushing too hard. That actually slows down strikes and kicks instead of speeding them up.

We engage opposing muscles that prevent us from optimally impacting the target.

Say you want to sleep, telling yourself you desperately need it. You've shorted yourself on this vital repast for a few evenings or even weeks of months, and you simply must have it. Now!

That's forcing matters, and it backfires.

How does forcing yourself to drink glass after glass of water, feel? Not so good, is it?

Forcing any naturally occurring bodily function typically produces nasty side effects.

And yet we still command ourselves to sleep.

I realize there are sleep gurus that hawk the benefits of selecting a sleep time, and then sticking to it. Supposedly, this is a means to achieving a minimum quantum of sleep every day.

But what if you're not tired when the appointed hour arrives? That ship can't leave the dock until you're fully on board.

So, what happens? You notice you're not sleeping "on time." This goal isn't being attained, leading to frustration, and that leads to more wakefulness.

A vicious cycle of unwanted sleeplessness is inaugurated, leading to the question, "What's wrong with me?"

To most questions, the simplest answer is usually the best and most accurate. This principle is called, *Occam's Razor,* if you want to look it up.

"I'm not sleeping because I'm not sleepy."

That is a perfectly reasonable, utterly simple, and generally applicable explanation.

You don't have a problem. You're simply not tired.

Your body knows it, but your conscious mind fights against it. So, what does your mind do?

It devises a way to exhaust you, if you're not going to get up and expend yourself in a more constructive or congenial way.

Then you worry. Worrying is an exhausting endeavor. It burns calories. It makes your heart pump faster, keeping you awake.

Finally, you give up on getting to sleep. This may take the form of bolting upright and bouncing out of bed. You might decide to clean the house or put your clothes on hangers.

Soon, you'll be doing the stuff that will tire you out. And because you are no longer striving for sleep, or as Mr. Miyagi would say, because you stop trying, you relax enough to hit the sack harder, faster, and without resistance. You're back to where you should have been to begin with.

When you put head to pillow your amount of exhaustion should be such where you're surrendering to the inevitable. You have so little conscious energy left that you have none available to wage any resistance.

As a wise sage, Jane Roberts put it in *The Personal Sessions, Book 4*:

"To solve a problem you begin to minimize its characteristics, diminish its importance, rob it of your attention, and refuse it your energy. The method is the opposite, of course, of what you are taught. That is why it seems to be so impractical."

Fighting non-sleep only adds to its influence over us. That which we resist, persists.

Turn your attention to other things.

Pick up a dictionary. Turn to a random page. Select the first word you see. Read the definition.

Go on to the next. Let your mind wander. Muse over meanings. Let thoughts cascade through your awareness, darting here and there.

Savor words you've heard, but you never had a meaning for.

Appreciate how you're learning with no specific impetus for completion and no time constraints.

Read more words. Whisper a few aloud.

Enjoy their strange sounds. Look at their provenance. Are they from Middle English, or from Latin?

Consider the people that uttered them and the times in which they lived. How did they dress?

What did they do for entertainment?

Did they ponder words and meanings, as well?

What were their days like? How did they feel as night fell?

They earned their rest, and so have you.

Drift off now. Your sleep is ready. There's nothing left to do.

Be Rich Now! Your Guide to Instant Wealth & Success

'm rich, and you can be, too. It's a choice you can make, right now.

A few days ago I was running errands, nothing special, when I felt a tingling sensation moving up my spine and spreading out to my limbs.

I felt serene and energized.

At that moment I knew everything was great, exactly the way it should be. I was aligned with my purpose in life, and I was calm and confident.

That is exactly what real wealth feels like.

I was rich. This I knew to the core of my being.

Later that day, checking my email, I found there was an unexpected note from a business associate suggesting we do a new deal together. It was good news, a confirmation of what I was already feeling.

Maybe my ESP tipped me off that something rosy was underway, before I read his note. In other words, I could have been I tingling because I was succeeding.

Like a radio, I was receiving a signal someone sent to me.

Or, I may have been broadcasting a signal of my own.

My delightful feeling might have sent a vibration out to my associate, prompting him to suggest a new venture.

You, too, can sincerely feel rich, this very second, by experiencing that tingle for yourself. You may only be a nap or a good night's sleep away from feeling as wealthy as you'd ever hope to be.

There have been times in my life when everything I touched turned into gold. Even my misses became hits.

For example, I invested more than I ever had in a mailing to promote a few of my seminars. I sent out more than 100,000 pieces. The postage, alone, cost a small fortune.

Thinking of it now I have to admit the mailer was ugly. It looked amateurish.

My seminars were not well attended. They managed to "make," which is to say we garnered enough registrations to earn back most of our expenses, but there was a slight paper loss I was going to take.

Then, two new clients stepped forward, right out of that ugly mailing. One client invested about $20,000 with me, which made the overall investment a modest success.

The second client invested about $330,000 with me over a ten-month period, making that overall marketing experience a big net plus.

From a career viewpoint, I was hot and no matter what that mailing did or did not do, I was going to remain hot.

Partly, I stayed golden because I wasn't anxious about success. Of course, I cared about delivering value, but I saw my ugly mailing as an experiment. And on one level, it was.

Instead of sending just one flyer into each company, I sent five, to various functionaries. Purposely, I over-mailed, hoping the redundancy would have a positive effect.

No one ever told me to do this. Nothing I had studied or learned to that point suggested this was an established, verified marketing gambit.

It worked, but in an unexpected way. Instead of getting more than one person from each company to sign up for my public seminars, these two clients decided it would pay off for them to have me conduct my programs in-house and to customize them for their firms.

One manager revealed that after receiving my mailing herself, four others staff members appeared with it as well. Seeing their genuine interest in my content, she hired me.

When you have the right feelings, wealth will come to you, even if it initially appears as scarcity. Sometimes, success can be disguised. It can be hidden in the absence of definitive feedback, in null results or even in outright failure.

Even precursors to success can masquerade as inactivity, as pauses in the action instead of bold strokes.

Sleeping is like this. It is like hitting the reset button so you can awaken to the wealth that is already at hand.

Where exactly is the wealth? Where does it dwell?

Many say it resides in a bank, in real estate holdings, in stocks and bonds, and in enterprise ownership.

This means that being wealthy is objective; something you can count.

I think being rich and having wealth are more *subjective*, a matter of attitudes, frames of mind, expectations, and those tingling feelings.

You could start your life as a trust fund baby and squander everything that was handed to you. Easy come, easy go, that's how it can work.

It is a well-documented and frightening fact that lottery winners, people that enjoy sudden financial windfalls, garnering millions, are likely to go broke in a short period of time after their winning numbers come up.

How can that be? In many cases these folks hailed from a background of struggle and privation. We might think they'll do the prudent thing and sock away most of their winnings in solid investments, setting them up for life.

They don't. They spend like crazy and are easy marks for scammers and long lost relatives seeking handouts.

They don't keep the money because they don't know how to be rich. Above all, they feel poor, still, even as their pockets are bulging.

You've heard stories about heroic moms and dads that scrimped, saved, and sacrificed to raise their families. "We didn't feel poor," their now-grown kids recall.

Somehow those parents made their dollars stretch. They lived better than their financial circumstances permitted because they wouldn't let their financial circumstances determine their feelings of abundance.

By so-called objective standards, they were crazy to feel rich when they hadn't a penny to spare. Compared to the billionaires that feel enough is never enough, who basically are emotionally insecure, enough will never deliver the satisfactions enjoyed by that family of super-modest means.

Don't get me wrong. I am not saying money has no role in producing happiness.

It can and it does, for many. And I hope you'll use this book to get more of that stuff if it can help you.

Doing this can require overcoming the impoverished thinking many of us have about money, contained in these old maxims:

- *Money is the root of all evil.*
- *You can't buy happiness.*
- *You have to step on a lot of other folks to get ahead, financially.*

These are false beliefs and excuses.

My view is that you should go ahead and earn a lot of money; more than you technically need, making you objectively rich.

Have that experience, and by doing so, earn the right to criticize it.

I am wealthy in college degrees. I earned five of them at good schools. Four are graduate degrees.

I am also a critic of the current management structure of most universities. I believe today's students should very seriously evaluate the costs and relative benefits of attending college the old-fashioned way.

The traditional route requires four to five years to earn an undergraduate degree, plus significantly more time and effort to get a law or medical degree.

There are better ways of doing it than the menu of fixed options presented by today's educational establishment.

I'm not saying you have to earn five degrees to form an opinion about their merit. But it doesn't hurt one's judgment to have been a part of the establishment as I have been.

Occasionally, when I enumerate my degrees for strangers, their jaws drop and I joke,

"I have a couple of degrees I'm not using, so if you'd like to buy one, let me know!"

Still, I feel wealthy-in-learning not because of those credentials and what I learned while completing them. I'm rich because I continue to learn on my own and I love the process.

The love of learning, with the time to learn, plus infinite resources at my fingertips, in libraries and online, is the source of my wealth. Happily, wealth of this type cannot be depleted. Let's repeat that.

True wealth cannot be depleted.

Seen this way you can appreciate the wisdom in movie producer Mike Todd's statement:

"I've been broke, but I've never been poor."

Being broke is being moneyless. Being poor is being hopeless. There's a huge difference.

To prove you can be rich now, let's count the ways. A great method is by making a gratitude list.

This concept sounds airy with the texture of cotton candy, but there's a deep dimension to it.

A small entry on my gratitude list is the fact I showed unusual restraint yesterday by staying off the gourmet chocolate chip cookies and moist crumb doughnuts.

I was rich in self-control, especially during this holiday period when we all get a free pass to be indulgent.

I'm rich in having the freedom to write. Can you sense what time I'm writing this segment? (4:41 AM.)

Does it show?

That's freedom, and worth being grateful for. We should celebrate being able to do what we do whenever and wherever we wish to do these things, whether it's as a profession, a calling, occupation, hobby, or goof.

I'd like to share this fantasy I harbored when my life revolved around the telephone, as a seller, an entrepreneur, and then a promoter of the medium's efficiencies, for both marketing and general business.

I would imagine I'd been magically dropped into a foreign country where I didn't know the language. All I had is a phone and international calling capability.

Would I survive? Would I thrive?

I believe I would. In fact, fueled by the adrenalin of the challenge, I'd probably succeed wildly and have a blast while doing it.

That's being rich in professional self-confidence. I appreciate and am very grateful for the fact that somehow, I would find a way. I could list 100 or even 1,000 things that I'm grateful for right at this very second. Doing so, I become rich in gratitude!

Harken back to what I said about wealth. It is never depleted. It is always accreted.

One act of gratitude spawns the next.

After you have finished compiling your own gratitude list, what you will find is an overwhelming sensation of tingling and well-being.

If only we can remember to make our lists on a regular basis!

This feeling is the key to abundance. You have it, now. You are it. You're flourishing.

Gratitude permits you to see the instant wealth that is at your fingertips.

As Buddhist nun, Pema Chodron says, "We're a heartbeat away from enlightenment."

I interpret this several ways. With our next breath we can awaken to our wealth. Inhaling gives us everything we need in order to live at this moment. Realizing that we have enough—enough oxygen, and enough bodily functioning to carry us forward—is an affirmation of life itself.

It is proof that nothing is missing in this interval in time.

What I call MIA thinking or missing in action thinking, robs us of our wealth.

Seeing life as the one big question, "What's wrong with this picture," and then answering it in countless ways, only promotes misery and poverty of the spirit.

Many are habituated to drawing up *ingratitude lists*. Who and what can we blame for our current state of lacking?

Here's a typical rant:

Let's start with our parents—were they messed up, or what? And why did they dare bring me into this most imperfect world? They should have known better. They were inept. Played hooky from parenting school. They were such embarrassments. And they certainly should have thrown flower petals and hundred dollar bills at my feet. If I'm screwed-up today it's because of them, 100%. I should have had Mike's parents. Now they were cool.

That one tops many ingratitude lists—bad parents. Next on the ingratitude list? I'm too:

- Short
- Tall
- Fat
- Thin
- Weak
- Dumb

- Smart
- Shy
- Bold

And don't forget, there's just a lot MISSING from my life. If I only had:

- More money
- More hair
- More talent
- More connections
- More education
- More time
- More energy
- More sex
- More lean muscle tone
- More motivation
- Then I'd be *fine*

Richard Alpert, also known as Baba Ram Dass, wrote a bestselling book back in the 1960's titled *Be Here Now.*

He was spreading the message that folks should appreciate "the pleasantness of presentness," which is a basic Buddhist insight. Maybe it is the most pre-eminent insight.

Part of the baggage of Eastern thought is the repudiation of worldly goods. Some people inter-pret this to mean if we can just let go of that need to drive a $150,000 Mercedes, and walk along with a modest begging bowl, we'll discover the path to Enlightenment.

I paid cash for a $150,000 car. It was a lemon. It turned me into a beggar. I begged the dealership to give me my money back, which they did.

I am not here to say you should spurn the goodies and trinkets life has to offer.

Have the experiences!

Find out what's they're about.

That car wasn't about speed, though it was fast. It was about the feeling I thought I would have, the one that screams inside and to your inferiors on the road, "I'm rich!"

Look at me. Aren't I cool? I have one, and you don't. I won!

However, dragging it to the shop incessantly because the pesky "check engine" light didn't turn off dampened my competitive fervor. I paid a ton for a car that had me perpetually riding in lesser loan vehicles.

So, I owned it, but I didn't. It owned me.

As you've heard, and maybe seen on TV, if you're successful you have an entourage, a supporting staff of nannies, landscapers, building contractors, Realtors, lawyers, CPAs, PR people, hair stylists, and yes, car mechanics that can't fix the electronics aboard the fanciest new rides.

What's the good part?

There actually is a good part, but it isn't what you think. It isn't in having all of the toys and the people to service and support them.

You have to go way back before they showed up to find the good part. In my fifth year of college teaching at a leafy Midwestern university, the type every young tenure-track professor desired, I was undergoing a personal consciousness raising.

I looked out at my rows of students, most of whom were children of the wealthy, and I realized they had a better trajectory in their future careers than I had in mine.

With BA degrees, not PhDs such as mine, they'd be welcomed to a world of corporate privilege and upward mobility.

I knew this to be true because I worked my way through college in sales and management with Time-Life, a very powerful company. And I earned far more there, double what I was getting as an Assistant Professor, eight years and three degrees later.

So, I hatched a plan to teach seminars by the day, aimed at businesses, instead of toiling by the academic year. I re-priced my talent and moved back to California.

One night, after I had been on the phone convincing Texas colleges to sponsor my one-day programs, I had this tingling feeling I've mentioned to you.

Although we occupied the worst apartment in the complex, the one directly over the racket of the garage gate opening and closing at all hours, I turned to my wife and firmly declared:

"We're rich!"

Bless her heart. She took me literally, thinking we won the lottery or that I found an abandoned mattress with millions sewn inside.

I explained this feeling I had that coursed through my bones and spinal column, that suffused my entire being with lightness and buzzing, indicating that wealth was ours.

"That's nice," she offered in reply, weakly.

At that moment, even if she doubted it, I knew I just had to keep doing what I was doing and the material manifestation would come in the fullness of time.

And it did.

But here's the fun part. Where did that wealth come from? And where did it dwell?

And what made it feel so intoxicating?

I can say this. It wasn't waiting in the showroom, disguised as a $150,000 car. It wasn't that first home we bought from the proceeds of a mistake.

What a story!

I scheduled a series of seminars with a university in Indiana. They were going to take my program region-wide, to Chicago, St. Louis, and Indianapolis.

I got them to experiment with a new concept. Why profit only from those that attend? What if we could also do well with those that could not attend?

I persuaded the school to insert an ad for audios containing the contents of the program as an alternative purchase. The price was $199.

The mailing to over 100,000 businesses in the region got out late. This impacted registrations at the St. Louis seminar, but we still were able to run it and the others.

They were successful.

Happily, more than 100 signed up for the audios. 90% of that revenue came to me. My cost was under $5 per set.

That's how I netted enough money to make a down payment on our first home in Southern California.

Back to my question: Where did that wealth come from? And where did it dwell? And what made it feel so intoxicating?

An accountant would say the wealth came from seminar and audio sales and from the equity the house accrued through the years, and the rental income it derived that paid off the mortgage.

Did it really come from there? Do you believe that? I don't.

Let's go back farther. The turning point was when I decided I could do better teaching by the day instead of by the semester and year. But at that time, it was only a hunch.

I had a little success, after I left conventional teaching and hit the stump with my one-day offerings.

But I was still struggling, financially. My California rent for a noisy apartment was three times what I paid in Indiana. When I bellowed, "We're rich!" there was no evidence to support that outrageous claim, except my feeling of wealth, that tingling sensation.

A thought, a feeling, an expectation, a goal, and above all, the belief that "It's possible!" can all play a part. This is a good place to discover where wealth comes from.

Just as enormous power resides inside the atom, that tiny, invisible-to-the-eye particle, unbelievable power resides in the MOMENT—in the NOW.

Be Rich Now says it all, because NOW is the best time to be rich. It is also the ONLY time in which to be rich. Repeat this NOW:

I'm rich.

I'm rich.

Now say it like you mean it!

I'm rich!

I'm rich!!

I'm rich!!!

That's better.

Let's cycle back to that notion of being "objectively" rich, wealthy in dollars and cents. Let's say at this very moment you're broke, behind in your payments, on the brink of bankruptcy.

Objectivists would say you have a money problem, and they'd be wrong.

Robert Schuller, the motivational author and speaker, says what appears as a money problem, isn't. He says:

"You don't have a money problem; you have an *idea* problem."

Dwell on that for a moment, and let's go back to the breakfast nook in my apartment when I declared, "We're rich!"

The problem seemed to be, while that new notion sounded good and it was wonderful I was tingling, we had no money to prove we were rich. Indeed, the absence of money said the opposite.

We were poor!

How do you get from poor to rich?

It's not by making the excuse that it takes money to make money.

You need an *idea* to get from poor to rich.

I already had one at the time. As I mentioned, I was teaching by the day instead of by the year.

Simple math told me if I did enough of it, I'd earn a big income with few expenses. Investing the surplus funds would make me wealthy.

But I needed the confidence to follow my plan to propel me into that objectified, wealth-verified future.

Where would that come from?

It comes from feeling wealthy, now.

We can call this *unconditional wealth*. It is subjective, a truth about your circumstances that only you can feel, for yourself. Your CPA can't fathom it, and you can't borrow against it or spend it, at least not now.

When I asked you to make a gratitude list, it was to engage a process for making objective, provable to you right now, the fact that you are rich.

I'm using an objective technique, list making, to engender a subjective understanding that *to-feel-rich-is-to-be-rich*.

Picasso painted a revealing portrait during his starving Parisian days when he was in his early twenties, titled *Bibi la Puree*. He had just returned to Paris and was preparing for his first exhibition. He presented a brash and bold new style of painting heralding a new era for the art world. *Bibi la Puree* features a famous clown, bum, lowlife, raconteur known to artists and dwellers of certain seedy Parisian digs. Ostentatiously dressed, Bibi is a parody of success, and the lack thereof.

Picasso is making my point about being rich. It isn't completely objective. It is subjective, too, and very powerfully so.

Pablo Picasso was one of the most original artists of the twentieth century. He was also a commercial success and individualist. At every age and stage, he was perennially young and perennially productive.

He proved you can, and MUST be rich irrespective of your financial means at any given time. His life is a great model for us.

There are five characteristics, operating together, that constitute what I think of as *The Picasso Principle.*

- *Originality*
- *Individualism*
- *Perennial Youth*
- *Lifelong Achievement*
- *Turning Trash into Treasure.*

There are many folks that manifest one or possibly a few of these attributes, but when we compare them to Pablo, they inelegantly mush their way through life. They're caterpillars, never becoming butterflies.

Unquestionably, Picasso lived a rich life.

We, too, can transform our potential into becoming outstanding human beings while thoroughly enjoying ourselves and appreciating those around us.

At the time of his death at age 91, Picasso left behind no fewer than 48,000 art works. Da Vinci is believed to have produced fewer than 100.

Frankly, I don't like all of Picasso's output.

There are work products in his famous periods, the Blue, the Red, and Cubism, while historically significant, that leave me wanting. So, his example isn't a glowing endorsement of his entire collection, but is it a positive acknowledgment of the fact that there are so many.

He succeeded wildly, on his own terms. He remained young until he died. His genius was acknowledged and celebrated during his lifetime.

What could be better?

He accomplished outsized things under the oppression of the Spanish Civil War and two world wars, centered in Europe.

He sired two children after age 70. In the 1940s this was practically unheard of, and it stands for the proposition that he did practically everything, his way.

Today, it's common to lionize those that "disrupt" the status quo, especially in business. Economist Joseph Schumpeter's notion of "creative disruption" illuminates how progress is a process that continually destroys the old ways while relentlessly creating new ones.

Long before this conception become popular, Picasso was brazenly disrupting the art world and those in the business of art. He declared:

"Every act of creation is first an act of destruction."

Artists and entrepreneurs have much in common. Above all, they are comfortable proclaiming:

"Here's how I see things. You should them my way. Here's what's missing."

Then they shower you with ideas and products that spring straight from their imagination.

To feel rich now, channel your inner Picasso.

Let's look at number five of the Picasso Principle, which is "Use everything and turn trash into treasure." A film about the artist followed him as he rummaged through a junkyard. Every now and then he'd stop to examine someone else's discarded item.

He wasn't hunting for anything in particular. He was simply seeing what was in front of him and deciding if he could any of it.

He was seeing without searching, scanning more than sifting. By the time he had emerged, he was holding some bent pieces of metal, probably made of tin, and a fragment or two of ceramics.

Picasso couldn't articulate what he was looking for, because it wasn't anything objective. Even if he started with a hunch about finding an object he could use, that notion regarding what he was after was bound to change before it presented itself to him.

This is akin to the notion found in the Chinese book of wisdom, the *Tao Te Ching*.

"The best travelers have no fixed plans."

In Picasso's meanderings, the best garbage sorties weren't really searches, at all. They were journeys without a destination.

You could say he arrived before he departed.

Picasso died rich, in objective, monetary terms.

But he was subjectively rich all along the way, even when his works were sold in Sears stores for only a few bucks each.

See it my way. Here's what's missing.

Sometimes, wealth is manifested in an independent spirit, one that says:

I Won't and You Can't Make Me!

About a hundred years ago an industrialist decided to do something very unusual.

He was staffing his assembly line and he wanted to attract the best workers he could get. So he sent out a call far and wide, that quickly was repeated by word-of-mouth to every corner of America.

He was willing to pay five times the average wage for factory workers. This was unheard of pay for that type of work.

Moreover, offering five times what nearby factories were paying was going to put excruciating pressure on other industrialists. When they heard his call, they went crazy.

"Why would he do it?"

"Doesn't he know this is going to ruin him?"

"Does this idiot want to put the rest of us out of business?"

"You must be crazy to pay people more than the next employer will."

"This dummy is going to launch a labor war!"

"He's a traitor to his class!"

They couldn't understand his thinking and concluded he was completely unreasonable. They pressured him to change his mind. Okay, you can pay more, but make the figure marginally higher, not five times higher! That was simply outrageous. As you might have guessed, there was sound reasoning behind his bold offer.

He wanted to recruit the best and if he paid the best wages, he felt he would realize this aim.

Those folks would make good, reliable products. They'd be likely to have fewer sick days, because for every working day they missed, they were losing a lot of dough.

And they'd work overtime, which was expected because the products they were making would be in demand.

Above all, if they made $5 a day instead of $1, they could afford to purchase their own products, the ones they toiled so hard and so proudly to build.

Henry Ford knew what he was doing, even if the rest of the industrial world thought he was missing some wing nuts.

He invented the modern American auto factory and his legacy continues, as does his name stamped on them.

This story is vintage, but it is as fresh as today and as cutting edge as tomorrow.

Wherever there is tremendous innovation, leading the charge are unreasonable people. Reason would have them not rock the boat. They would go-along-to-get-along, doing what they can to not offend their peers. Ford didn't just make factories hum with astounding productivity. Literally, he put horses out to pasture. He made them obsolete, along with carriages and buggy whips.

He destroyed the old order. As balladeer Joni Mitchell sang decades later, Ford and his type "paved paradise and put up a parking lot."

We are a car culture, largely because of this one exceedingly unreasonable man.

As George Bernard Shaw noted in his play *Man and Superman*, "The reasonable man adapts himself to the world: the unreasonable one persists in trying to adapt the world to himself. Therefore all progress depends on the unreasonable man."

Most books, especially of the self-help variety, instruct us to buckle-down, to cut away our idiosyncrasies, to conform. We're encouraged to harness our wayward natures, to fit in.

But this is not the way of progress. At best, it is a formula for stasis, for perpetuating the status quo. It teaches us, for instance, to work like machines, to replicate and not to originate.

Get more (of the same!) done in less time and we call this productivity. Do well what shouldn't really be done at all, and you'll be esteemed by the bozos that ordered the irrelevant work to begin with.

At worst, the status quo message has us chasing old dreams with obsolete methods.

For example, chances are very good that you're reading this book or listening to it on an audio device without the physical book or a dedicated playback machine in front of you.

It exists in the computing cloud, and you can enjoy it in a number of convenient formats.

Which is great. But what if, as an author, I insisted my books exclusively be printed on paper and bound into tidy volumes the ways books used to be manufactured? That might work with a select audience as a retro publicity stunt. But I'd be putting the vast majority of my potential audience out to pasture.

Independent bookstores have been shuttered because of Internet sales, and that's a cultural loss. But the gain has been astonishing.

Just last night I decided to read *Look Homeward, Angel* by Thomas Wolfe, and *The Sun Also Rises*, by Hemingway. I didn't have to break into my local library after hours or find one of the few open bookstores in Southern California.

I found these volumes through Project Gutenberg, a nonprofit repository of old titles that have been uploaded to the Internet. This is an astonishing resource. I've been catching up on the great books that I missed reading in my early years, and it has been a real pleasure.

The idea of Project Gutenberg, to scan millions of titles and make them instantly available to the masses, is outrageous in its ambition and scope. It is also destructive of the old order.

It is helping to make folks like me "rich," and scholars and everyone worldwide, more effective by several orders of magnitude.

This is like a $5 day wage, but for the mind. Make that a $10,000 day because it is so vast and powerful.

This is progress, and it is anything but reasonable because it threatens the old way of doing things, including how profits were made and distributed.

Albert Einstein said:

"If at first, the idea is not absurd, then there is no hope for it."

I'm here to say we have to interrupt our old patterns or we'll become helpless and hopeless. We won't maintain the existing order, because it is inherently entropic. It is wearing down and wearing out.

We have to actively replace it, purposely pushing it into obsolescence. We must practice saying no to the indoctrination and regimentation that is forced upon us.

In every crucial arena, from formal education to how and where we earn our daily bread, we need to say, "I don't want to, and you can't make me!"

Dissatisfaction isn't a sign of impudence, a childish and churlish retreat from responsibility. It should be seen as a trigger, a goad to get somewhere past good, and well into better.

Procrastination and other forms of avoidance aren't defects. They're signaling that doing certain robotic or preprogrammed things isn't working for us. Our routines could be perfectly rational in the short run, like working at a lifeless, breath-stealing job, day in and day out.

But these rational routines need to be examined and jettisoned even at the risk of temporary anomie and chaos.

In the 1976 movie *Network*, a news broadcaster snaps on the air and yells: "I'm mad as hell and I'm not going to take it, anymore!"

"Go to your windows" he implores his viewers, and shout out the same line:

"I'm mad as hell and I'm not going to take it, anymore!"

In that spirit I'm encouraging you to unleash your inner maverick.

When you are asked to sacrifice your sleep and to deny your deep biological need to enjoy true wealth, say: "I'm not going to do it, and you can't make me!"

Be a Local Hero and
Know True Wealth

Being unreasonable or offbeat is a way to make an astonishing life and world-changing progress.

Local Hero is a gem of a movie that speaks to this idea. Set in the 1980s, it tells the story of a Houston based oil company bent on rapid, global expansion.

The young fellow dispatched to purchase some land in remote Scotland is played by actor, Peter Riegert. Riegert arrives and discovers all kinds of quirks and anomalies.

The bed and breakfast hotelier is a jack-of-all-trades. He is the local person who will be negotiating the deal to secure the land rights for the oil company.

This takes assembling a lot of individually owned properties, owned by some who are grateful to turn over their land for money.

But there's a holdout. He's a curmudgeon living on the beach in a dilapidated shack, accessed only by a flimsy ladder.

Riegert tries to win the fellow over, pitching all of the benefits that relinquishing his land will provide.

The codger isn't having any of it. He points out that he'll just have to replace this spot with another, there is no place more beautiful and restive, and the beach gives him his living and his daily routine.

Riegert insists that the offer is too attractive to refuse. The man won't have to comb the beach or fish for his dinner ever again.

He'll be free!

When asked exactly what the oil company will do with the land once it is theirs, Riegert tells him about the huge refinery they'll build.

"No, I don't see that happening here," the senior citizen says with the gentle but firm glare of an oracle.

This charming tale is something you should see. It is far more textured than I have described.

It stands for several ideas we're touching on.

That elder, the beachcomber, has everything, from his viewpoint—beauty, nourishment, a job to do, caring for the beach and finding sustenance there. All of these payoffs are his now, on a regular, uninterrupted basis.

Why would he sell out, just to exert himself reconstructing them somewhere else, especially when there is no other spot on earth like his?

Riegert shows him photos of the world's most beautiful beaches, where he can relocate, but the harder the Riegert pushes the more the beachcomber recoils.

What's ironic about this movie is it came out at the time I was commuting to Houston for a mega-consulting project that would take place over two years.

I was a lot like the beachcomber. I lived in California at the time in a beautiful home, in a beautiful location. I was spending five days a week in a distant city so I could earn a fortune that would enable me to live in the same exact home in the same location where I already was.

On the road I was living in a large, one bedroom apartment suite at the Four Seasons Hotel, renting it by the month, about as opulent as travel can get.

Tunnels connected my digs to a shopping mall and health club. The concierge even scored Rolling Stones tickets for me when the venue was already sold out!

But at home, I already had what I was seeking. I was already rich, without realizing it. I was living in clover, but the clover wasn't good enough. The voice that kept going off in my head said, get more, get more, get more, ever more. It was as if Peter Riegert had visited my beach and sold me on the idea of giving it up! In Little League, there was a kid on my team who was going to graduate to Pony League after the season concluded. Our coach needed a new catcher to take over Jimmy's duties.

He asked me if I wanted to learn the position, and I said, why not?

Jimmy spent hour after hour teaching me the basics. I practiced crouching, throwing out runners at second and third base, and even learned a thing or two about helping pitchers get through games.

Jimmy was also a surfer, and it was this keen interest that led him to Hawaii, after he reportedly turned down an athletic scholarship to attend USC.

I heard Jimmy was parking cars in paradise at night after hitting the waves by day. Friends would chuckle as they regaled the story. He sounded like the perfect flake.

Parking cars, who did that? But there's an expression that I've found to be true. If you can make your way to paradise, paradise will support you.

Jimmy parked cars so he could pursue his passion—surfing. Surfing was his wealth.

Many saw him was as a bloke who lacked ambition, doomed to be broke. Maybe he was penniless after paying his bills and maybe not. But in a very real sense, Jimmy found his way to be rich, NOW. Many people postpone living the good life because they believe they have to suffer to get it. This is folly.

For years, I used to joke with restaurant hosts that I wanted a seat with an ocean view. I made them chuckle, especially if we were in a landlocked place in the Midwest.

Of course, there were times when I could get one, especially when visiting Hawaii, or driving over to Malibu.

But alas, these would be one-hour rentals, at best.

Having stated my desire for an ocean view, maybe a thousand times, I finally listened to my own quip and took it seriously.

I really, really wanted an ocean view.

Of course, living at the beach is very expensive. Several years ago, when I was doing a major consulting contract in Florida, I spoke to an executive who told me about his incomplete mission to buy a home with such a sweeping vista.

"My wife and I traveled all along the west coast and we couldn't even find a beach shack for less than a million dollars," he lamented. (Make that two to ten million, today.)

Of course, he was speaking about owning a property, which is the goal of most folks.

Going out of country didn't make the prospect of an ocean view more feasible. As I write these words, you cannot legally own a beachfront property in Mexico, if you are an American. You can get a long-term lease on it, I believe up to 99 years, but it will not be completely yours, unless the law changes.

This really bothers people, in spite of the fact that 99 years is probably way long enough to occupy any property on this planet, given our life expectancies.

Instead of finding, leasing, and pleasantly occupying a place in paradise, we dash that dream as financially unattainable. Remember, Jimmy found a way to get to and live in Hawaii, sustaining himself by parking cars. Getting the title to a piece of property was probably out of the question for him.

Flash forward a few decades. I heard he's still in Hawaii, running charter-fishing tours. And he's undoubtedly happier and richer than most.

Thy Rest Be Done!

I am not an expert on things religious, but I do know something about the Sabbath.

It is a day of rest for many who adhere to Judeo-Christian religions.

Frankly, I never contemplated writing about it, because as I see it, religion is deeply private. Having one, not having one, is your choice and you don't have to announce or affirm what your beliefs are, at least if you are an American or a citizen of most modern Western societies.

Recently, an article ran in *The New York Times*, titled *What if the Real Act of Holiness Is Rest?* Speaking of observing the Sabbath, writer Margaret Renkl recalls her childhood and how her grandma firmly observed a day off from worldly matters.

Her essay reminds me that resting, which can certainly include napping and sleeping, is not only a physical act, which is frequently how I treat it in this book.

It has the potential to be deeply spiritual, in keeping with holy dictates.

I may be going out on a limb by suggesting that setting aside the Sabbath for resting is also one of the most practical rules established by religion. It is a built-in prophylaxis against many of the woes and temptations that constant busyness can usher in to our lives.

Look no farther than to our constant commentaries on social media using today's technical devices. These are envy-based vortexes, inducing us into vices, summoning our nonstop attention and commitment.

They also focus us on materialism, and I would argue more specifically on consumerism. By aggrandizing the buy-now impulse, they subtly encourage the accumulation of debt and eschew the postponement of gratification.

People who get rich aren't constant spenders in the same way that physical fitness pursuers cannot be constant eaters.

There is a role for fasting as part of a smart diet and fitness routine. I say this not only for the purpose of temporarily reducing calories. The more important function of fasting is to restore to us a feeling of self-control.

Fasting sends to our minds and bodies the empowering message that we are in control of our intake. If and when we want to adjust it, we have the will to do so.

The Sabbath introduces a regular work-fast. It creates a needed separation between the ordinary, the mundane, and the covetous nature many of us can succumb to and the elevated, the detached, the transcendental.

Ironically, by turning to matters other than the commercial we're more apt to return from our restoration with renewed commercial capabilities and insights.

Some of the highest earning people in the world observe the Sabbath.

Much is being made today of the concept of emotional intelligence which translates roughly into having and using people skills.

Is it possible that there is such a thing as *spiritual intelligence*, as well?

I would characterize this as the self-wisdom to know when you need to shun the profane and embrace the profound, to seek to elevate your thoughts, feelings and appetites to a plane that delivers something different, something deeper.

Being materially rich is nice, but being spiritually rich can be even better.

Lest we believe this pursuit is exclusively or especially made by Westerners, there is ample literature suggesting that Eastern sages have been in touch with Sabbath-like precepts for ages.

The *Tao Te Ching*, an ancient book of wisdom attributed to Lao Tsu asks:

"Can you wait until your mud settles?"

This pithy question has the power to snap us out of our monkey-minds. In Zen Buddhism, "not-doing" is considered a highly evolved practice and spiritual achievement. I quoted California's ex-Governor Jerry Brown for famously stating, "Sometimes, not-doing is the highest form of doing." Brown was a former seminary student and more than a casual acolyte of these notions.

"Do no harm" is the literal translation of the Oath of Hippocrates, which every physician unofficially subscribes to.

I would say we're not very successful at refraining, and our impulse-control in this regard grows worse, prompted by technologies, especially instant communications.

Pausing the noise, shutting off the constant cacophony of voices seeking to catch our attention, can be a conversational fast. It is needed to clear our minds of blockages and pollutants.

Devoting an entire day to a Sabbath could seem to some, excessive. Given our greed for speed, couldn't we cut that back to a mini-Sabbath, maybe a half-hour or so?

Can't we get the same benefit from what is becoming widely popularized—mindfulness training?

I don't think so. To borrow from Baba Ram Dass's book title, mindfulness helps to "Be Here Now." Being fully at work when you're at work is a good thing. And being fully away from work is also to be desired. It is just possible the ancients knew this when they handed down the concept of a Sabbath, and its year-long version—the sabbatical.

These days, being fully away is the trick, not being fully here. We're here 24/7 and it is precisely this surfeit of availability that keeps us from achieving wealth—both monetary and spiritual. If we were to adjust Ram Dass' title to suit my purpose, and to reflect journalist Renkl's thesis, it would read: "Be Rested Now!"

Poor or Rich, A Princess Is Always A Princess

———∞———

There's a beautiful scene in the movie, *A Little Princess*.

Stripped of her privileges by the mean Mrs. Minchin and consigned to a musty attic and practically starving, the heroine, Sarah Crewe awakens to see a sumptuous, steaming hot banquet laid out in sterling before her, manifested from the chilly air.

Instantly, she is rich again, or perhaps she is richer than ever before. Having suffered humiliating privation has given Sarah depth and sensitivity that might have remained latent had she not struggled to survive.

This poignant and surprising scene, this respite from ruin, is filled with questions. One of them is:

What makes us rich?

Sarah slept a pauper and awakened to splendor. Did her repose cause this blissful result?

In literature and in psychological archetypes, sleep is a metaphor, standing for a period of incubation. It says we need to be surrounded by darkness before being aroused by the light. A period of inactivity, dormancy, is the precursor to arousal and rising to greatness.

Through deprivation, we earn our redemption of abundance. Being empty is needed before we can be full.

Most heroic stories follow this sort of narrative.

The weak or poorly functioning protagonist is reluctantly called on to make a journey, in which she encounters multiple obstacles, her character forged, put on trial by fire, and challenged, repeatedly.

If she accomplishes her goal, she wins the day and possibly becomes a legend. Even if she fails, she does so with full commitment and possibly selfless sacrifice, and prevails through a noble failure.

We have an everyday sense of what it means to be rich. Money in the bank, lavish estates owned and manicured by others, titles and miscellaneous other holdings and perquisites—these are the earmarks of being rich, correct?

Not so fast, while wealth managers might identify these assets as desirable in their pursuit of clients, what we're searching for in these pages is not only that.

We're looking at sleep as a purposeful void, an absence of affluent articles, tangible trinkets and other fêtes and fetters.

Sleep is the container that we allow to shape us and prepare us for regular consciousness. It is a mold. If broken or cracked, it fails to provide us with the cohesion needed to face everyday waking realities and challenges.

Did the banquet make The Little Princess rich?

Was it by way of being provisioned, suddenly supplied with a surplus of goodies, too many to consume right away, was this the signature of sinecure, of success?

One of the ideas that we consider here is that you are, as she was, already rich.

Being unaware of this fact makes you unconscious. You're the sleeper, needing to be awakened to your actual status. The banquet is an outer manifestation, a materialization of the wealth you have inside of you.

She was a Princess, and called such by Mrs. Minchin who had previously admitted her with open arms to the private girls' school Minchin managed. This was when the student's affluent father paid tuition before he was conscripted, then went missing in action and was presumed dead, in World War I.

Mrs. Minchin mocked her with the same moniker, "Princess" when the young lass was penniless and required to scrub the school floors, to earn her keep as a mere laborer.

But there was something in the girl, deep empathy, or what we would today inadequately call emotional intelligence, that made her an informal leader; one looked up to by her privileged peers, even as she toiled in tatters in front of them.

We come to see that it is the intangible qualities that are a wellspring of wealth.

Sleep is the cocoon in which these precious sensibilities are given the opportunity to accumulate. The boast of the honest, the moral, the humane individual comes to mind when he or she says, "At least I can sleep at night."

The person who cannot sleep well may be haunted by feelings that he or she is not living rightly. Sleep is the calculator that tallies the daily receipts from our waking experiences.

If our feelings don't balance, like numbers that don't match, there is a price to be paid. There is a cost.

Some researchers speak about the idea that we can incur "sleep debt." If we don't get our solid share of rest, usually seven to nine hours per night, we are faced with an emotional, intellectual, and physical deficit.

If our sleep debt grows worse, with continuing mismatches between our required rest and our actual rest obtained, we wear down and ultimately break down.

Scientists have said the absence of sleep is a greater threat to our well being than the absence of food. We can survive longer without food with less damage to ourselves than we can by going without sleep.

Can a person, perennially in sleep debt, or frequently in and out of it, be considered rich?

I say no.

My dad knew a fellow who lived in a modern palace, who was fond of boasting about his money habits. One day he pointed to a table that contained savings passbooks that tallied his bank balances.

"See those over there?" he asked. "There are 100 savings books with $10,000 in each of them," which at the time was the amount the federal government would insure.

Quickly, my dad calculated he was looking at a million dollars, available in cash, upon demand to this fellow. In those days, this was quite a sight.

I'm here to say if that man slept fitfully, or less than his appropriate amount, as informed by his native predisposition, he wasn't rich.

Rich, in my lexicon equates to being at peace.

In the middle of the Princess' suffering, despite her fall from financial grace, she slept with the angels, who ultimately rewarded her with the ultimate gift, the return of her lost father.

So, as I've said a few times, you are rich now, right now, at this very moment. Not knowing it is the cause of suffering, a symptom of which may be fitful or insufficient sleep.

If you believe going sleepless, pulling what students call all-nighters, is necessary to grow wealthy, you're wrong.

Feeling lousy makes you feel impoverished. And from this cranky, groggy, listless, and resentful emotional place it is supremely hard to become materialistically rich.

Let me say it this way. "Poor today, but I'll be rich tomorrow!" isn't a practical prescription for happiness, in spite of the fact that some psychologists say postponement of gratification is a sign of maturity.

It didn't work for me. After years of self-denial and sacrifice I reached the financial plateau that I had set out to scale. My reward was a deep feeling of emptiness, an anti-climax.

I realized it wasn't my personal balance sheet of holdings that equaled wealth or the baubles and status objects I had and could yet acquire. My wealth resided in my self-confidence, my grit, my willingness to challenge myself, and my craving for lifelong learning.

I was rich long before I was rich, and it was being rich already that made me rich.

Ironically, when I translated this into objective, materialistic targets, into terms that were universally verifiable instead of remaining internal, intrinsic, and intangible, I missed the mark.

Let me repeat, "Poor today, but rich tomorrow" doesn't wear well and isn't a recipe for sustained success.

"Rich today, rich tomorrow and always rich!" is a far better perception of what wealth is. You don't need to go get it. You need to stay and have it.

All you really need is your sleep and the values that effortless, refreshing and rewarding repose reflect about the overall life you're living.

Your marching order is: feel-rich-now. Give yourself the pleasure and tranquility of appreciating that wealth is in you.

Before long, it will probably surround you, as well.

In Summary–
Snooze & You'll Cruise

There is credible research that validates the connection between good sleep and affluence, bad sleep and poverty.

A good night's sleep isn't the effect of having money in the bank. It is the necessary prerequisite to putting that money in the bank. The work ethic doesn't do it, but a rest and rejuvenate ethic can. Sleep is the last thing we think of underpinning success. Because it is so obvious, it is invisible. People wrongly believe that incessantly long working hours are good for individuals, their companies, and for the economy.

The evidence points to the contrary. An in-depth article titled, *The Complicated Relationship Between Sleep, Health and Poverty*, on the advocacy website

Global Citizen.org addresses how sleep is related to poverty:

> People who sleep less earn less. In fact, one study found that one more hour of sleep per night can lead to a 16 percent higher salary annually in the US (about $6,000). This is huge evidence that sleep has a major role in explaining income gaps in society!
>
> This makes sense when you think about it. Poor people tend to face more stress in their daily lives; stress leads to poor quality of sleep; poor quality of sleep compromises a person's ability to get through their day, which leads to more stress, which makes this cycle even worse. When you throw the health problems into the mix, this becomes a toxic recipe for hard-to-escape poverty.

What's ironic is we lionize those in business and industry that seem to sacrifice sleep for achieving greatness. Yet, as I've pointed out, the facts betray this correlation. Let's re-examine some famous examples of sleepers and non-sleepers.

Edison, the genius behind so many inventions, is said to have given up a full night's sleep. Yet he napped, incessantly, reaching REM sleep, the deepest and most creative kind, more times in a 24-hour cycle than most average achieving folks.

Einstein dreamed his relativity theory; he did not "think" it. He said, "I never came upon any of my discoveries through the process of rational thinking."

Admittedly, he didn't *Think & Grow Rich* as the classic title put it. He slept and grew rich, dying a wealthy man. His heirs continue to earn approximately $15M a year, passively, in licensing revenue from his contributions and persona.

Contrast these snoozers with Elon Musk, a contemporary creative force behind Tesla and Space X among other ventures. He is famous for boasting that he sleeps very little, often curling up under his desk.

That eccentricity led to his being investigated and fined for fabricating an insomniac's tweet for taking Tesla private, with funds ostensibly lined-up for that purpose.

Businesses push employees to work super-human hours, yet fail to understand the price they are paying for sleeplessness. Reportedly, healthcare costs are $3,500 per year higher for employees that have a sleeping problem.

As you've seen in these pages we are defeating ourselves by sacrificing sleep, especially if we believe by doing so we'll improve our income and wealth.

That adage, "You snooze, you lose," is 100% wrong.

When it comes to being truly healthy, wealthy and wise, the expression should be, "You snooze, and you'll cruise!"

As we've seen, the quality of your life increases with being well rested and refreshed.

Gains in income are greatly offset when we sacrifice sleep. I've shared numerous examples from my professional life that detail how big paydays can be negated by onerous working hours.

Business travel, whether 500 miles away or around the globe, is arduous enough with missed flights, bad weather, countless delays, and jet-lagged insomnia. Ultimately, the dollar premium we earn, the battle pay we receive, is eroded and destroyed by the fatigue premiums we are forced to pay.

When all you want to do on a weekend is catch up on your shuteye, and you have no inclination or time to spend your earnings, something is terribly out of balance.

Sleeplessness is the leaking pail. We fill it at waterside, but by the time we return to the spot where it can refresh us, the water has escaped.

Our solution is to rush faster to and from the water. But we can't keep up with the loss.

The problem is in the design of the pail, and on an even higher level it pertains to our lack of a passive water supply, something we can tap and shut off at will.

We have designed our waking and sleeping lives in ways that make us poor instead of rich.

We've substituted an external clock for the all-important internal one, the biological clock.

This isn't new, this regimentation, compartmentalization, and trivialization of our time. It dates back to the Industrial Revolution, when clocks were installed in town squares, to alert people to the start and stop of the working day.

The simple fact is, and you may have surmised this from my tone and text, taking back possession of your sleeping hours is reclaiming all of your time. You are exercising sovereignty over your whole self, your physical, mental, spiritual, and material being.

It is a radical change in your consciousness and behavior.

Doing this, recovering ownership of your days *and* nights, is as revolutionary an act, as daunting to the status quo as was dumping tea into Boston Harbor.

I may not have made this clear to this point.

When your employer coyly insists on tapping into your downtime, your private hours, your natively endowed needs for rest and rejuvenation, he or she is stealing from you.

Say you're paid, to use round numbers, $1,000 for 40-hours, this seems to work out to $25 per hour.

But if it takes more than 40 hours, each added unit of required time waters down that salary.

Say it takes 60 hours to do that job. It's a job-and-a-half for a one-job paycheck. Suddenly, your pay is $16.66 an hour, not $25.

If you have to catch-up on merely eight hours of schedule slippage, including a modicum of missed sleep, assuming you can physically do it, which many scientists say you cannot, that's a 48-hour week you're working. In money terms, you're being paid $20.83 per hour.

Plus, you're sacrificing much of your weekend, just to pay back your sleep debt from the period that came before.

To mangle an old laborer's song that said, "I owe my soul to the company store," you owe your *snore* to the company store. There's really no way to get paid fully for that.

I am especially concerned because this sleep theft resulting in sleep debt is really quite subtle and generally undetected by victims.

What do we tell ourselves when we've worked overtime and we're totally bushwhacked on Satur-days or Sundays?

I guess I'm not getting any younger! Suppose I need a few more energy drinks to get me through the day.

Wrong. Irrespective of your age, you should be enjoying the proper quantum of sleep that will enable you to awaken fully refreshed, be productive when you do awaken, working up to your standards, and allow for the sorts of side projects that can make you rich.

Let's talk about those side hustles for a minute. Through our hobbies and tinkering we not only do something pleasurable. If we're good at it, we can sometimes fashion a healthy second stream of income from it.

I was a full-time, tenure track assistant professor with a duty to research, prepare, deliver, and grade papers for four different courses, simultaneously. It was a huge burden.

Somehow, I found the time to conceive of a short, one-day class for business. I offered it at Cal State Los Angeles during a break from my Midwestern teaching duties.

It was fun, it paid some pin money, and it alerted me to the notion that I could offer more of these programs, back in Indiana and elsewhere.

Within a few months I left that regular college teaching job and exclusively did my one-day seminars, finding myself at 35 universities, from Hawaii to New York. I earned more than 10 times the ordinary professor's pay, and I was independent, financially and otherwise. The side gig became the regular gig, and that spawned other peripheral activities such as keynote speaking and authoring.

Whatever I did, I always allowed time to rest and recuperate. Sometimes this entailed not traveling for years at a clip, because I felt exhausted.

We need to become commanders of our own clocks.

When I left the tenure-track teaching job, which was designed to be a job for life, I took my life back.

Today, there is a lot of publicity about how robots and software are replacing people. Instead of accepting this fact, people are trying to work faster, at breakneck speeds to rival robots. They're transforming themselves into machines, but unlike their competitors, we can't easily be upgraded, swapping out faulty and worn parts.

I say this: Don't even try to emulate machines, though your employers may stupidly entreat you to do so.

In days of yore, when men worked most industrial jobs, Peter Drucker called these unrelenting occupations, "widow makers." Literally, doing these jobs put workers into pine boxes.

What are the drivers of sleep deprivation, sleep debt, and sleep theft?

Greed and fear are at the top of the list.

A young couple decides to buy a motor home to save on hotels when they take their growing family on vacations.

This means he needs to work overtime at his job selling heating and air conditioning equipment to consumers. Evenings and weekends are repurposed to earning the added dollars it takes to make the new RV payment.

She has to keep her job in teaching, of course, to help pay the other bills.

But they don't have the time to use the motor home because of the added need to pay for it. Plus, he's always feeling physically zapped by the time he gets a day or two off from work.

If this sounds like the plot of O. Henry's classic short story, *The Gift of The Magi*, in which the love struck couple each secretly sacrifice their prized possessions to buy Christmas items for the other, you're catching the essence of what I'm saying.

What can be worse than tying yourself down to an eight-year RV loan and to working incessant overtime, all preventing you from enjoying that RV?

Or, for that matter, tethering one's spouse to a job simply to pay for status objects and expensive toys you and they don't need. While this is happening you are warehousing your kids in day care or after school care, that will never deliver the goods like parental attention and a close relative's loving kindness.

Do the math. Is that second income really getting you where you want to go? Given the costs of above mentioned warehousing, and nannies, and the avoidance costs of not-parenting, plus taxation, how much happiness are you bringing home with that second check?

Allow me a brief history-of-economics digression.

Immediately after World War II, the United States had captured 70% of the gross industrial output of the world. Japan, Germany and other countries sustained extraordinary damage to their manufacturing capacity and supply chains.

For about 20 years, one income in America bought a house, with the help of the GI Bill. It put two cars in every garage that wanted them. It clothed, fed and schooled millions of newborns.

The American economy did this miraculous trick on a single earner's paycheck. That breadwinner might have had at most a high school diploma, and many did not have even that. And many who did receive a college education were also able to get there with the GI Bill.

Prospects were bright and earning capacity was unquestioned because America was the industrial engine of planet earth.

I don't need to tell you that the world rebuilt itself and now if you want that home it typically costs over $400,000 instead of $15,000. Car loans are stretching to seven years, because prices keep going up and earning power doesn't keep up.

Two entire generations are sensing that their economic lives will not be as easygoing as their parents' and grandparents' were.

Still, there is a choice to be made. Keep chasing those material goods, and in doing so keep driving up prices, well beyond your reach.

Or, change your material aspirations. Henry David Thoreau said the cost of a thing is how much of what we call "life" you are willing to trade for it.

Let me put it this way, in keeping with the theme of this book.

How much sleep and tranquility are you willing to forego by trying to buy and keep a house that you cannot afford?

Will you trade tranquility and innate wealth for an RV, or third car, or private school tuition, or student loan debt?

Please appreciate the fact we discussed earlier: You simply cannot *consume* your way to riches. Most things that you'll buy lose most or all of their resale value.

Regarding this point I had a lucky conversation with the president of a car-leasing firm I worked for straight out of college. His family were pioneers in the business, in which he grew up.

Therefore, Jim had a lot of credibility.

"Gary, what is the single biggest expense in a person's life?" he asked.

Mulling it for a few seconds, I replied, "A house?"

"Nope, that's what most people say," he retorted. "It's their cars."

How could that be, I wondered.

"Cars are an expense. Financing them, repairing and maintaining them, and then selling them for a fraction of their initial value, and doing this maybe 20 times in your life, that costs a fortune," he explained.

"Houses go up in value," he added for emphasis.

Generally speaking, buying things of all kinds, and not just cars, is costly. Furniture notoriously loses its resale value, unless you're speaking of antiques.

So, you won't buy your way to riches.

Much is written about how much Americans are in debt. A trillion and a half bucks are owed in student loans, and an amount nearly that in car loans.

But there is good debt, which I detail in another book of mine, *Stiff Them!*

Good debt includes money borrowed to obtain assets that do appreciate, such as real estate. Say you own a string of apartment units. Rents will be raised periodically, putting more profits into your pocket.

And while there are maintenance costs and vacancies to be filled, generally apartments will give you passive income. Countless folks have amassed fortunes by patiently building portfolios of real properties.

I love that term, *real properties,* when speaking of real estate. It reminds us that most other forms of physical property are comparatively unreal.

Generally, real properties gain value 24 hours a day, seven days a week, and 365 days a year. Owners can sleep well, knowing they are resting on valuations that almost inexorably rise, even while they personally slumber.

Don't look for your labor alone to make you wealthy. Riches will come to you through other means, and the best ones are relatively passive.

Psychologist Dr. Srully Blotnick studied the careers of hundreds of people, tracking their ups and downs over the course of 20 years.

Who got rich? And how did they do it?

In his book, *Getting Rich Your Own Way* he doesn't say you must invest in real estate—at least, not directly.

He says wealth can be earned through almost any occupation. Here's how it happens.

You fall in love with plumbing. Plumbing fascinates you so much that you keep up with every trend, reading all the trade publications you can find.

You join trade associations and get to be known in the industry as the preeminent troubleshooter in the plumbing field. You're tapped to offer consulting advice on tough projects, and you earn exceptional money.

In the meantime, you are offered a partnership stake in the plumbing firm you work for. That becomes more and more valuable as the firm expands, opening more locations.

You invest your surplus earnings in real estate and in stocks and bonds, not worrying much about the highs and lows of the economy.

Before you realize it, your personal wealth runs into the millions of dollars.

It wasn't your goal to get rich. Wealth was a byproduct of falling in love with plumbing and sticking with it for the long haul, becoming an expert in what you loved.

Essentially, that's the path most of Blotnick's wealthy research subjects followed.

They got into a field that interested them. They stayed with it, developed their skills, were gradually paid more and more, and invested the extra earnings in other, generally passive ways, such as in real estate.

All were surprised by how their wealth grew.

Those that started out with the explicit goal to get rich didn't fare so well, according to Blotnick. They flitted from one field to the next, never quite developing the skills and knowledge base to exploit their potential advantages.

Another interesting and significant footnote is that in the long term there were no significant differences in the wealth earned by high school versus college graduates.

What Blotnick didn't discuss was the overall happiness of his subjects, those that grew rich versus those that didn't. I can't help but infer that the financial winners not only achieved a huge payout from their careers; since they remained vitally involved in them they were probably happier and more eager to go to work each day that were the money-seekers.

I'm guessing they slept better, partly because they weren't in a rush to get rich.

DON'T HEED THE SIREN SONG OF SLEEP DEPRIVATION

At this very moment I'm studying an ad that appeared in a recent magazine, which says,

You Eat A Coffee For Lunch
You Follow Through On Your Follow Through
Sleep Deprivation Is Your Drug Of Choice
You Might Be A Doer

An online freelance marketplace sponsored the ad. It shows a sallow but still attractive young woman. It celebrates "lean" entrepreneurship and is part of a campaign, "In Doers We Trust."

This ad was critiqued in a New Yorker article by Jia Tolentino, appearing in 2017, *The Gig Economy Celebrates Working Yourself To Death*.

The article recalls how a very pregnant Lyft driver squeezed in accepting another fare moments before giving birth. Lyft used the tale as a device to demonstrate the driver's heroism and the company's ability to deliver an income earning opportunity in an instant.

These examples are the very antithesis of what we have dedicated ourselves to convey in this book.

Incessant busyness, just-in-time birthing, sacrificing your health, endangering others on the highway because you are sleep deprived, relinquishing your life to the demands of employers and even mere gig providers, are the sorts of sacrifices that will not make you rich.

Quite the opposite, they are calculated to impoverishing you while enriching exploiters.

Stop allowing others to determine what your work-and-life-balance should be. These lifestyle decisions shouldn't be left to self-aggrandizing zealots. They should come from within.

FIGHT BACK AGAINST SLEEP SHAMING.

Fight back against what I call *sleep shaming*. This is when your nearest and dearest relatives, roommates, and friends deride you for being lazy or selfish or a slacker because you are heeding your own biorhythms.

Don't con yourself into thinking you can go into sleep debt, interminably. Incessant sleeplessness, sleep interruption, sleep sacrifices, are simply a different type of anorexia.

You are starving yourself of the vital essence you need to sustain your very life.

Lest you think I'm making up the idea that today's businesses are sneakily trying to steal your sleep, look at this comment on the job posting website Indeed.com, from a former employee of a company that is advertising job openings:

Pros—Flexible schedule, hard rewarding job. Great customers!

Cons—Worked around the clock.

Putting the two together, what is this job rater saying?

Good news: There is flex time! Bad news: Choose any 24-hour period of the day you want to work.

Beware: This is a pact with the devil, working around the clock.

I've had some very interesting epiphanies after engaging in sleep starvation. There is a point that

I reach, of almost giddiness, feeling that I'm getting away with murder, so to speak, by denying myself shuteye. This has been a frequent perception at the end of very taxing consulting assignments, usually far from home where I have commuted in an out on a weekly basis.

About my bone busting routine, I think, "This isn't so bad. I'm on top of this. I can handle it."

And you can almost time this with a stopwatch, that super-heroic sentiment comes a day or two before my mind and body crash and burn.

One symptom is that I get sick.

I realize it won't take a mere day or two in order to recover my stamina. It's going to take a lot more than a week or two, or even a month or two.

I need to go cold turkey to break the addiction to self-denial. These incidents are not helping me—all of the jet lag, the shortened temper, the dangerous racing to, through, and from airports, along with all the accompanying stresses.

They're killing me. And from a monetary standpoint, they don't enhance wealth; they threaten it.

I have "mini-retired" several times in my life, removing myself from the road and from a lifestyle with everything I could want at my fingertips, except rest and relaxation. Remember, I've had concierges that got me impossible-to-find Rolling Stones tickets and rarified interactions with movers and shakers.

But I've also sheared years from my career at a time, simply to restore sense and stability to my life. Every time I have done this it has entailed a financial retrenchment, a dissipation of earnings, and a scaling back of spending.

The words of Edward Albee come to mind, expressed by a character in his play, *The Zoo Story*:

"Sometimes it's necessary to go a long distance out of the way in order to come back a short distance, correctly."

The long distance he's referring to is what I see as leaving behind our true natures.

I traveled the world to prove I could get rich when it was returning back home, a short distance correctly, that showed me I was rich where I was before the journey began.

We don't prosper by suppressing our humanity, and by training ourselves to subvert our native impulses and imperatives. When we do, we achieve a false prosperity. It vanishes sooner than we expected.

Sustainable wealth depends on sustainable health.

We started this book by noting that the richest person on earth, Jeff Bezos, is also one who properly values his sleep.

Judging from interviews with him that I've seen, he also values his overall health. He is a fitness devotee and when asked what he would like written on his epitaph, he quipped:

"Here lies the world's oldest man."

I don't mind saying I admire him because of the long-term view he takes of building a business and a rich life.

Repeatedly, he has chosen growth of his flagship, Amazon, over quarterly or annual profits.

His space exploration company, Blue Horizon, is a venture that Bezos realizes will require a multi-generational effort to bring to fruition. You simply cannot have the attention span of a fruit fly and build organizations for the ages.

TRANSITIONING INTO SLEEP SOBRIETY— A 30-DAY INACTION PLAN

In this book I've skirted around the edges of calling our impoverishing habits everything under the moon. It's time to indict them for what they are.

Bad sleep, and the everyday choices that lead to it, is an *addiction*. It isn't an acute condition. It's chronic.

Therefore, it is going to take some time to cure.

And you will need to clear the decks and make time for a saner, more sober sleep routine.

Ideally, you would take some vacation time to start. I suggest taking time off of work.

What? Am I nuts?

Well, you'd be calling in sick if you went into drug rehab, and sleep rehab requires some safe space in which to explore and practice lifestyle alternatives. Plus, you are sick if you're sleep stressed and missing your proper quantum.

If you like you can call it a vacation and take vacation time, if you have accumulated it.

But don't pack your bags. Don't go on a trip. Stay right where you are, because your everyday abode is where you'll be hunkering down into dreamland after the initial 30-days have passed.

You do appreciate how exhausting most conventional vacations are, correct? They are anything but restful. We pack into them so many new sights and sounds and places and foods that our routines are completely upset.

Vacationing-in-place for the purpose of becoming sleep-sober, is the diametric opposite.

Choose an exercise that you haven't been doing. You'll be adding this to any other workouts you're doing.

It could be Tai Chi, the gentle martial art of slow, graceful movements. Or, if you prefer, it can simply be walking around the block a few times, every day.

There are You Tube videos on nearly every exercise you can imagine. Watch one, but don't allow yourself to think you have to be a professional or invest in a new outfit to do what I'm saying.

Your new exercise serves several purposes. For one thing, it tires you out in a good way.

This predisposes you to getting more sleep, to falling asleep faster and to having a more restful sleep.

Drink more water than you normally do. This will cleanse you.

Listen to your body. Eat only when you're hungry, not at the usual times. If you can, cut back on the junk food.

Instead of reaching for a third cup of coffee to stay wired, take a nap after your lunch or at some point in the afternoon.

It will feel decadent to some and delicious to others. How long should your nap be?

You're on vacation, so who cares?

Still, as a general guideline, there are folks that find 30 minutes refreshing while others require 60–90 minutes. You'll quickly determine what works well for you.

What if you can't disconnect enough to enter full slumber? Then **turn this time into a meditation.** Become aware of your breathing. Take deeper breaths.

Allow your mind to think happy thoughts. Observe the fancies and fantasies that come and go without judging them.

Count butterflies. Wow, look at all of those colors! They're merging into a kaleidoscopic tapestry.

You're getting sleepy, now.

See?

Researchers tell us that the blue light emanating from our phones and computers interferes with our ability to fall asleep. So, on your **sleep-cation**, try to disengage from screens an hour or two before you go to sleep at night.

Listen to soothing music instead of the agitating kind. Composers Debussy & Ravel are good. The classical guitar and the lute can be very relaxing.

What you don't want to do is to turn your sleeping routine into work!

Yesterday, I checked out a book that just appeared in my local library titled, *How to Not Always Be Working*, by Marlee Grace. It's a small gift book.

The gift of the book is its very title.

Appreciate that we're turning nearly every activity into work and we need to create zones where we're off the clock.

What is *not* work? The author lists eating pie, sitting on the beach, taking a shower, reading a book, and a few other activities.

I'm adding sleep to this list, and taking a sleepcation is your announcement to yourself and to the world that you're restoring this essential rest time to its proper place in the pantheon of human activities.

During your 30-day routine change you'll need to alter some other things. I suggest less TV binge-ing. Don't check your email or social media accounts after working hours.

Become less available to others and more available to you and to your inner drives and rhythms.

Imagine a mud-filled glass. As you agitate it, the mud coats the inner surface making it impossible to see through it. When you wait for the mud to settle, the glass becomes clear.

As I noted earlier, the ancient book of wisdom, *Tao Te Ching*, asks: "Can you wait for your mud to settle?"

This is what changing your sleep routine will accomplish.

It will give you clarity. Your mind will become less populated by rants. Whispers from your inner being will become audible to you, suggesting you try this or that.

Connecting with your deep self, or should I say, connecting with your sleep-self will lead you to appreciate the occupation and career you currently have. Or, it will signal you need to make an appraisal, perhaps distancing yourself from what you're doing.

By coming into alignment with your subcon-scious, with your natively endowed wisdom and bio-rhythms, propitious paths for your development will emerge.

You'll grow richer in self-acceptance, in self-guidance, and if you want to attract material wealth, you'll be open to that as well.

As the *Tao* says, when your mud has settled the right thing will arise by itself.

Sleep well, and prosper!

Afterword

I've enjoyed writing this book for a number of reasons, and I sincerely hope you will profit from it, mentally, spiritually, and materially.

If you'd like to reach me to discuss your goals or your company's objectives, try the following email addresses or phone, bearing in mind they change from time to time.

I coach individuals and do corporate consulting and speaking so don't be shy. Please reach out and I'll reply promptly.

You can also find me on LinkedIn and stay in touch that way.

In the meantime I wish you all of the best.

—Dr. Gary S. Goodman

gary@drgarygoodman.com
drgaryscottgoodman@yahoo.com
garysgoodman@gmail.com

gary@negotiationschool.com
(818) 970-GARY (4279)
(818) 970-4279